GNVQ: is it for you?

GNVQ: is it for you?

Second edition of the guide to General National Vocational Qualifications and GSVQs, the Scottish equivalent

Windsor Chorlton

Foreword by Gilbert Jessup
Deputy Chief Executive and GNVQ Director,
National Council for Vocational Qualifications

Student Helpbook Series

HOBSONS

CRAC

Acknowledgments

The author wishes to acknowledge the help of the following people:

Helen Aylett City and Guilds, London
Penni Blythe South West Association for Further Education and Training, Taunton
Anne Marie Chapman, Linda Kelly Scottish Vocational Education Council, Glasgow
Judith Compton, Universities and Colleges Admissions Service
David Harris Dorset County Council Education Department, Dorchester
Richard Hewlett Gloucester College of Arts and Technology, Cheltenham
Gilbert Jessup, Karen Jackson National Council for Vocational Education (NCVQ), London
David Moyes, Carol Turnbull Dumfries and Galloway College of Technology
Tom Storey, Chris Nother, Jennifer Thompson The Purbeck School, Wareham
Ian Thorington, Catherine Hughes, Belinda Singleton Guildford College of Further and Higher Education, Guildford
Linda Wyatt Ferndown Upper School, Ferndown
Thanks also to all the students who helped in the development of this book.

These materials have been developed with the help of John Tate (BTEC), Ursula Russell (RSA) and Malcolm Deere, Head of Academic Services and Development Department, UCAS. The materials have also been reviewed by the National Council for Vocational Qualifications (NCVQ). Thanks are due to Iain Grant, Publications Editor, SCOTVEC.

 © Hobsons Publishing PLC 1994

ISBN 1 86017 017 X

A CIP catalogue record for this book is available from the British Library.

CRAC

The Careers Research and Advisory Centre (CRAC) is a registered educational charity. Hobsons Publishing PLC produces CRAC publications under exclusive licence and royalty agreements.

Printed and bound in Great Britain by Clays Ltd, St Ives plc, Bungay, Suffolk.
Typeset by MFK Typesetting Ltd, Hitchin, Hertfordshire.
Cover artwork by Lesley Bisseker
Text illustrations by Jon Riley
Text design by Leah Klein

Ref. L218/E/7/qq/A/JF

Contents

Foreword

Although GNVQs are still relatively new, they are already making a major impact on education in the UK. Following the piloting of the qualifications in 1992–93, GNVQs became generally available for the first time in September 1993 – just over a year ago. As we start on the second year, the registrations indicate that as many as 150,000 young people are starting on GNVQ courses. This represents about one in four of all 16-year-olds in the country! And all the indications are that the proportion taking GNVQs will grow to half the population within the next few years.

This book provides a very readable account and a fair description of what GNVQs are about. It captures the excitement and enthusiasm that the new courses have generated amongst both students and their teachers. This, best conveyed in their own words and with the liberal use of quotations throughout, is what brings the book alive. The book also recognises the problems teachers and students have faced in these early days in getting to grips with the many new features of GNVQ. A great deal has been learned from the early courses which is helping to improve GNVQs and the quality systems which support them. Guidance and learning materials, not available in the early days, are now building up rapidly in all subjects and will help teachers and students on future courses.

The message we are getting from teachers and students all over the country is that GNVQs are hard work, but the effort is worth while. GNVQs are certainly not a soft option. It has now been officially confirmed by school and college inspectors that the standard of student's work of the Advanced GNVQ is on a par with A-levels, and that of the Intermediate is up to grades A–C of GCSE. It is now widely reported that GNVQ students are more confident and better able to plan and organise their own work, and are better at communicating their ideas, than other students of their age. This has been achieved by making core skills, including personal skills, central requirements in assessment – something no qualification has ever done before.

A recent report by schools inspectors who looked at GNVQ courses in over 170 schools in 1993–94 confirms:

'Students' responses to GNVQs have been overwhelmingly positive. Their chief sources of satisfaction are the degree of independence they achieve as learners, the collaborative relationships with their teachers and the breadth of scope the courses offer them.'[1]

Gilbert Jessup
Deputy Chief Executive and GNVQ Director
National Council for Vocational Qualifications

November 1994

[1] *GNVQs in schools 1993–94: Quality and standards of General National Vocational Qualifications, Office for Standards in Education, 1994, page 6, paragraph 16.*

Introduction

❛ GNVQs contain features that employers and higher education say they want. They are broadly based, coherent and academically rigorous. They build on the best features of current vocational qualifications.... And they are flexible. Students can accumulate credits towards the final award, and can retake tests if necessary. This will ensure that these demanding qualifications are manageable. Students can take GNVQs alongside GCSEs, A-levels or AS. This style of qualification will tap a pool of talent that has been hidden for too long. ❜

Secretary of State for Education, 1993

A few questions to ask yourself

❑ Do you want a vocational education that will prepare you for a job or for further vocational training?
❑ Do you hope to go on to higher education but also want a qualification that will be valued by an employer?
❑ Are you unsure whether you want to go into a job or into higher education? If so, do you want to take a course that lets you keep your options open?
❑ Do you realise that GNVQs – especially at Advanced level – are not 'soft options'?
❑ Were you able to cope with your GCSE coursework?
❑ Do you like the idea of working independently, sometimes carrying out projects outside the classroom?
❑ Are you prepared to take responsibility for organising your own learning?
❑ Can you work well as a member of a team?

If you answered 'Yes' to at least a couple of these questions, then the General National Vocational Qualifications or GNVQs offer an option worth considering.

Two students who did choose the GNVQ option were Sarah and Robert. Here are their stories.

Sarah's Story

I chose Advanced GNVQ in Business along with my English A-level, as it offered excellent progression routes into higher education and employment. It enabled me to focus upon a vocational area and gain a qualification equivalent to two A-level passes, as well as having the opportunity to achieve Merit or Distinction which relate to the higher A-level grades.

'GNVQ offered a style of learning more suited to my needs, enabling me to work at my own pace. Much of the study relies on individual investigations which have developed my skills of research, planning and evaluation. The setting of personal targets has been essential, as is the negotiation of my achievements with my teachers. Throughout my studies I have developed the core skills of Communication, Application of Number and Information Technology within a business context. All work I complete for the GNVQ is accredited and tested as I progress, and provides a portfolio of evidence recording my achievements.

'When I leave school, I am going to further my education and hope to become a teacher of the upper primary age range. I believe my GNVQ studies have provided me with a firm foundation in terms of knowledge and a variety of skills which will be extremely useful to me in the future.

Robert's Story

I'd been thinking about working in the hotel business, but to be honest, I wasn't sure what I wanted to do. I got two GCSEs, so A-levels weren't on, but I didn't fancy going straight into a job. I could have done a course at college, but that's 40 minutes away by bus, and my parents weren't too keen on the idea. My teachers suggested I take Intermediate GNVQ in Leisure and Tourism and also resit maths GCSE. When the course was explained, it appealed to me. I liked the idea of being assessed for work I'd done myself. I'm not much good at exams.

'At first the work took a bit of getting into, but once I started the assignments I really enjoyed it. It's more like real life; you do practical assignments on your own or in groups. I also did work experience. I worked for two weeks as an assistant manager at a hotel. That gave me information on health and safety regulations which I needed for some of my units.

'There were some things I didn't like about the course. It took me a while to understand the language [of the programme specifications]. I also had trouble with the core skills – particularly Application of Number. But we were given special lessons, which helped.

'Although there aren't exams in GNVQs, you have to do end tests for each unit, and they were difficult. Some of the questions were so long that by the time I got to the end of them, I'd forgotten the beginning. I failed the first two, but passed them second time round. My teacher said I should try for a Merit grade, but I still haven't finished all my units, so I'll be happy if I get a Pass. You have to concentrate to get the work done.

'Was it worth while? Yes. I wish there'd been more work experience, but I have a much better understanding of the hotel business than when I started. I also passed my GCSE maths, so I'm glad I stayed on.

'I thought about going on to Advanced, but decided against it. After the summer I'm starting as a trainee with a big hotel chain. They were impressed by the work I'd done and offered me a place straight away. Without GNVQ, I'm not sure they would have been so keen.

Why GNVQs? Information for students, parents and teachers

Since 1990, the number of teenagers staying on in education after the age of 16 has risen by about 20 per cent. Many of these extra students are studying GCE A-levels, AS and GCSEs, but a large number are taking General National Vocational Qualifications. Introduced in September 1992, GNVQs are now offered in schools and FE colleges throughout England, Wales and Northern Ireland. A broadly similar qualification, the General Scottish Vocational Qualification, is available for Scottish students.

In the year GNVQs were introduced, nearly 9,000 students in more than 100 centres took the new qualifications. The following year, another 82,000 students signed up for GNVQs at 1,423 centres. In 1994, the number of students who chose the GNVQ option rose to more than 150,000 – about one in four of all 16-year-olds.

Clearly, the new qualifications have struck a chord with teachers and pupils alike, but what exactly are they, and how do they differ from other courses? In brief, GNVQs:

- cover broad vocational areas such as Hospitality and Catering, Leisure and Tourism and Manufacturing
- are aimed mainly at full-time students in the 16–19 age group, but will be offered to younger students and can also be taken by adult learners
- are already offered at three levels to cater for students with different abilities and aspirations (eventually there will be five levels)

➨ help develop the aptitudes and knowledge which
  employers say they want
➨ provide an alternative pathway to higher education
➨ include core skills – personal, transferable skills, such
  as the ability to communicate effectively
➨ allow students to keep their options open
➨ allow students to accumulate credits progressively.

For many 16-year-olds, GNVQs have been the answer to
the problem of having to leave because the courses offered
were unsuitable.

    What we needed was something which could be taken
to a variety of levels, which was a real alternative
to A-levels, but without the dependence on end-of-course
examinations. We were looking for a course which would
motivate students, as well as being seen by them
as meeting their needs. GNVQ seemed the answer to
our prayers!

A school in Northumberland

    I had already started applying for jobs when I was told
about GNVQ in Leisure and Tourism. I'd always
been interested in sport, so I thought I might as well give it a
go. I really enjoy it. It's different from A-levels – more
practical, less academic. You don't spend all your time
copying or making notes from a book. You do a lot of your
research outside school, investigating the local economy,
finding out how the leisure industry works. It's a good
course.

A 17-year-old GNVQ student

In GNVQ programmes the emphasis is on active learning,
with students carrying out projects and assignments that
cover vocational units as well as the core skills of numeracy,
literacy and computing. Students agree targets with their

teachers, who measure their progress by assessing their work against written specifications. The material collected by students is kept in individual portfolios. There are no end-of-course exams, but students take tests for each of the vocational units and must pass all of them to achieve the full award. Individual achievement is recognised by a grading system, with students able to achieve a GNVQ at Pass, Merit or Distinction.

The formula has proved an attractive one. Students say that GNVQs:

- stimulate their interest
- allow a welcome degree of control over their learning
- foster self-confidence.

However much you might enjoy a GNVQ programme, the crucial test of the qualification is its value to employers and higher education institutions.

Because Advanced GNVQs – the highest of the three levels – were designed to provide an alternative pathway to higher education, much attention has been focused on the question of whether they would square up to GCE A-levels as university entrance qualifications. An answer was provided when the first Advanced student completed her programme, gaining a Distinction in Art and Design and being awarded a place on a BSc course in Textiles at the Bolton Institute of Higher Education.

Of the other 905 Advanced students from the first phase who applied for higher education studies through the Universities and Colleges Admissions Service (UCAS), nearly 800 were offered conditional acceptances. That's a success rate of about 85 per cent, compared with an average of 76 per cent for students with GCE A-levels.

Although 22 per cent of the successful candidates had taken one or more GCE A-levels/AS courses in addition to GNVQ, most students gained university places on the quality of their GNVQ work alone. According to one senior educationalist, 'the likelihood is that before long roughly one in three entrants to HE will possess a GNVQ.'

How GNVQ students are faring in the employment market is less clear. This is partly because it is harder to track their progress after they have completed their programmes. The majority of GNVQ students taking the two lower levels are going on to other further education courses, including Advanced GNVQ. Although GNVQ isn't designed to teach work skills for a particular job, it should improve students' employment prospects and choices in their chosen area. It does this in several ways:

➤➤ by developing the general skills, knowledge and understanding required within the vocational area

➤➤ by developing the core skills of numeracy, communication and information technology required in most occupations

➤➤ by providing most students with some relevant work experience

➤➤ by fostering out-of-school links with local businesses

➤➤ by developing students' self-reliance, initiative and motivation

➤➤ by giving students experience of different occupations within each vocational area, making it easier for them to make an informed choice about the correct area for further training.

Many initiatives have been taken to promote GNVQs among employers. These are discussed in chapter 7.

General background

Before looking at GNVQs in more detail, it's worth considering why the qualifications were developed, and why they have been backed strongly by government, business organisations and higher education.

To compete in a sophisticated and rapidly changing global economy, a skilled and flexible workforce is essential.

According to the Confederation of British Industry (CBI), 'the UK needs, at the very least, a skilled and competent workforce on a par with those of its main competitors. Yet international comparisons give no cause for comfort. British employees tend to have fewer and lower-level qualifications than their counterparts abroad.'

Many 16-year-olds turn their backs on further qualifications because they aren't attracted to the academic courses which are all that many schools and FE colleges offer. As many as 40 per cent of students who start GCE A-levels either don't finish or fail. Yet even students who do well at GCE A-levels may start work with few of the skills essential to a well-run business.

Speaking of GCE A-levels, a science correspondent wrote: 'Qualifications at that level carry no guarantee that their holders have any of the skills and qualities which employers seek – including such mundane and old-fashioned virtues as honesty, reliability, neatness, a good speaking voice, unambiguous handwriting, evidence of manual dexterity and aptitude for practical work.

'At a more sophisticated level, A-level provides no

evidence of the ability to work in a team and to co-operate with others, or of a wide range of communications skills...'
[*New Scientist*, 20 March 1993]

The CBI agrees. 'Detailed expertise in one narrow area will no longer be enough', it says. 'Broader occupational competence is now required.' And that, the CBI believes, can best be gained by students taking a vocational course, or by mixing a vocational programme with academic studies.

The problem is that for many years vocational qualifications have been widely regarded as inferior to GCE A-levels, traditionally, and almost exclusively, the direct route to university.

In this country we have always failed to give status to the practical as compared with the academic and professional careers. The next generation must be able to decide between academic and vocational training without distinction or reserve.... But if the vocational route is to have equal status, we must offer a range of qualifications that is both wide yet at the same time easily recognised, understood and esteemed.

The Prime Minister, 1992

GNVQs have been designed to bridge the divide between academic and vocational qualifications. First proposed in the White Paper of May 1991, *Education and Training for the 21st Century*, they were conceived with ambitious targets. By 1996, the government wants 1,500 schools and colleges to offer at least two GNVQs, and hopes that by that date one in four 16-year-olds will be starting GNVQ programmes.

GNVQs for 14- to 16-year-olds
From 1994, acting on the Dearing report, schools will slim down the National Curriculum for 14- to 16-year-olds to

occupy about 60 per cent of the timetable. Mandatory subjects are limited to English, maths and a single science, plus short courses in a modern foreign language and in technology. Physical education, religious education and sex education are compulsory, but are not examined. Subjects like history and geography are optional.

Some 40 per cent of the time is available for studies outside the National Curriculum, and GNVQ is highlighted as one of the '*major new options*' that can be offered to pre-16-year-olds. Some schools with special facilities or industry links may also offer National Vocational Qualifications (NVQs) – qualifications designed to teach actual work skills for particular occupations. Opening up the vocational pathway to pre-16-year-olds brings England and Wales into line with other European countries.

Because Foundation and Intermediate GNVQs both cover the ground of about four GCSEs, it would be difficult to take either of the complete programmes without crowding out other studies. It's possible that some schools would offer a full programme by using time outside the National Curriculum, but in practice most pre-16 students would take a Part 1 GNVQ, probably consisting of three vocational units plus three core skills units from Foundation or Intermediate GNVQ. If they wish, they would then continue towards the full award post 16. Some students would choose to take only one or two units; these would be credited and recorded on the student's National Record of Achievement.

There is some overlap between GNVQ core skills and GCSEs, particularly in maths, which raises the possibility of students gaining awards in GCSEs and GNVQ units for the same course.

You may find that GNVQs are not on offer in your school at Key Stage 4. This is because the National Council for Vocational Qualifications (NCVQ), the body that sets standards of GNVQ delivery, strongly advises that only schools with the necessary resources and staff trained to deliver vocational education should offer GNVQs. Within a year or two the qualification should become generally available to students under 16.

A quick guide to GNVQs

In 1992, the year GNVQs were introduced, they were offered in five vocational areas:

- Art and Design
- Business
- Health and Social Care
- Leisure and Tourism
- Manufacturing.

In 1993, three more GNVQs were introduced:

- Construction and the Built Environment
- Hospitality and Catering
- Science.

In 1994, another five GNVQs were phased in:

- Distribution
- Engineering
- Information Technology
- Management Studies
- Media: Communication and Production.

These 13 GNVQs will be generally available from the academic year 1995–96.

By 1996, the number of GNVQs will have increased to 15. The table overleaf summarises their phased introduction.

With the exception of Management Studies, which is an Advanced programme, all GNVQs will be offered at three levels after their pilot year.

☞ *Foundation level* is a one-year programme for students who may have no previous qualifications. It

TIMETABLE FOR PHASING IN GNVQs			
Areas	**1994–95**	**1995–96**	**1996–97**
Art and Design	G	G	G
Business	G	G	G
Health and Social Care	G	G	G
Leisure and Tourism	G	G	G
Manufacturing	G	G	G
Construction and the Built Environment	G	G	G
Hospitality and Catering	G	G	G
Science	G	G	G
Distribution	P	G	G
Engineering	P	G	G
Information Technology	P	G	G
Management Studies (Advanced only)	P	G	G
Media: Communication and Production	P	G	G
Land-based Industries			P
Performing Arts			P

P: Pilot year; G: General availability to all centres

is the first step on the GNVQ ladder and has been designed to let students sample learning in more than one vocational area.

☛ *Intermediate level* is considered to be of comparable standard to four GCSEs at A–C grades and will probably take one year to complete.

☛ *Advanced level* is equivalent to two A-levels and will normally be offered as a two-year programme.

A fourth level, comparable with degree standard, has been proposed, and there is even the possibility that a fifth level, equivalent to a higher degree, may eventually be introduced.

NATIONAL FRAMEWORK OF QUALIFICATIONS		
HIGHER DEGREE	GNVQ5	NVQ5
DEGREES	GNVQ4	NVQ4
A/AS	ADVANCED GNVQ	NVQ3
	INTERMEDIATE GNVQ	NVQ2
GCSE	FOUNDATION GNVQ	NVQ1

16
GCSE
14   KS4
KS3
KS2
5   KS1

The diagram on page 13 shows how GNVQs fit into a proposed national framework of qualifications. Although other qualifications will continue to be available in specialised areas, the government intends that GNVQs, together with NVQs, their purely vocational equivalent, will become the main national provision for vocational education and training.

Responsibility and aims

Responsibility for developing GNVQs has been taken by the National Council for Vocational Qualifications (NCVQ), which also ensures that standards and quality are maintained. The three awarding bodies offering GNVQs are:

- The Business and Technology Education Council (BTEC)
- The City and Guilds of London Institute (C&G)
- The Royal Society of Arts Examination Board (RSA).

All the awarding bodies have extensive experience of devising and administering vocational courses.

Improving quality

Any major new educational initiative will have some teething troubles, and GNVQ is no exception. Although GNVQ is probably the most heavily assessed and evaluated educational programme available in this country, quality and standards in the early years were not always consistent. In response to its own findings and reports by outside bodies, NCVQ and the awarding bodies are taking measures to improve the quality of the programmes and to ensure that the necessary standards are applied in every GNVQ centre. Steps include:

- working with the awarding bodies to improve guidance to GNVQ centres
- publishing a series of booklets, *Assessing students'*

work, showing examples of students' work in each area to help convey the standards expected
- publishing guides and booklets on the assessment and delivery of core skills
- providing guidance on grading
- taking a central role in improving external verification, including the sampling of student's work by subject specialists
- improving the reliability and consistency of tests by adopting common external tests
- increasing the number of optional and additional units to meet the needs specific to employment routes or higher education programmes
- training teachers to familiarise them with the styles of learning associated with GNVQs
- supplying specialist teachers when necessary
- simplifying the language of GNVQs and clarifying the tasks required of the teachers and the students
- advising centres on the amount of time that should be given to GNVQ programmes.

This last move reflects the concern felt by NCVQ and other organisations at the fact that many of the first student intake, particularly at Foundation and Intermediate levels, did not finish their programmes in the recommended time. There were special reasons why the failure and drop-out rates were higher than expected, and these are explained in the following chapters. But it does appear that an important factor was the failure of some students and teachers to work to a realistic timetable.

It's only fair to stress that the first students and teachers were pioneers venturing into unexplored territory. For GNVQ candidates following in their path, the route is more familiar – pitfalls and all. And the goals – whether employment, further vocational education or higher education – are both clearer and brighter, making the journey well worth while.

1 How a GNVQ Programme Works

> GNVQ is about achieving outcomes. The prime words are "elements", which tell you the outcome you have to achieve, and "performance criteria", which describe what you have to do in order to achieve it.

GNVQ tutor

By the end of this chapter you should know:

+→ what a GNVQ is and how it works
+→ why schools and students like GNVQs
+→ what you will do on a GNVQ programme
+→ exactly what you need to do to gain a GNVQ.

The structure of GNVQs

The structure of every GNVQ is modular – that is, it is made up of a number of units (the higher the level, the more units) which together cover skills and processes relevant to the particular vocational area.

Most of the units in a GNVQ are called vocational units. Some of these are mandatory – you have to do them. Some are optional – you choose from a range of options. Among the mandatory vocational units in Intermediate Business, for example, you have 'Business organisations and employment' and 'Consumers and customers'. At the same level in Art and Design, the mandatory vocational units include 'Visual language representation' and 'Explore others' art and design work'.

All GNVQs also include three mandatory core skills units, at the appropriate level (Foundation, Intermediate or Advanced):

•▸ Communication
•▸ Application of Number
•▸ Information Technology.

These units are designed to test your application of personal skills which are essential in nearly all occupations, and in life in general.

Requirements

Although the basic structure of GNVQs is the same at all levels, the higher the award, the more demanding the programme.

In order to gain the full award at Foundation level, you must complete nine units – three mandatory vocational units, three optional vocational units, plus three mandatory core skills units. Because Foundation students may not have decided which vocational area they might wish to specialise in at higher levels, they are allowed to choose their optional units from the different vocational areas available at their centre.

At Intermediate level, you must complete nine units – four mandatory vocational units, two optional vocational units, plus three core skills units.

At Advanced level, you must complete 15 units – eight mandatory vocational units, four optional vocational units, plus three core skills units.

A summary of the mandatory vocational units for all the GNVQs currently available is outlined in chapter 2. The mandatory core skills units are outlined in chapter 3.

Each vocational and core skills unit sets out a number of requirements. For example, in the Intermediate Business unit 'Business organisations and employment', you are asked to:

•▸ explain the different types of private and public sector business organisations

➻ investigate business organisations and products

➻ investigate the UK employment market.

The requirements for each unit are quite precise, but they don't tell you what you must do in order to meet them. This is where you and your tutors can use initiative and imagination.

Evidence

To satisfy the requirements, you have to produce evidence gained from projects and assignments – activities which may range from interviews and surveys to role-play and work experience. It's a bit like working towards a Duke of Edinburgh award.

Although each mandatory unit is the same for all centres, schools and colleges may tackle them in their own ways. So, for example, a group of Leisure and Tourism students at a further education college collected evidence towards the unit 'Planning for an event' by organising a parents' evening, while a group of school students taking the same programme organised the school sports day.

Assessment

The evidence you collect is assessed by your tutors. *Continuous assessment* is the main process by which your performance is measured.

There are also *externally set written tests* for the mandatory vocational units. Designed to test your general knowledge and understanding of the vocational area, they consist of multiple-choice questions lasting about an hour. If you don't reach the required standard first time, you will be given the chance to repeat the tests.

Credits

When you have satisfied all the requirements for a unit and passed the *unit test*, you will be given a *credit*. The unit credit is a qualification in its own right and also a partial qualification towards the full GNVQ award. Even if you do not complete a full GNVQ programme, you will receive a certificate listing the units you have achieved. If you do pick up the rest of the units later, you will then be awarded a GNVQ. It doesn't matter how long it takes you to complete the programme.

On achieving the full GNVQ award, your work will be assessed again. If it shows a level of performance above the basic requirement, you will be awarded Merit or Distinction grade.

Learning about the programme

When you enrol for a GNVQ, you won't be thrown in at the deep end. Before you get down to the real work, your tutors will tell you everything you need to know about your programme. Some schools and colleges issue students with handbooks that explain the basics. This chapter has a similar purpose. It takes you step by step through:

•→ Timetabling arrangements
•→ Vocational units

- Elements
- Performance criteria
- Range
- Evidence indicators
- Projects and assignments
- Documentation
- Portfolio of Evidence
- Assessment
- Unit end tests
- Grading
- Support systems.

Induction programmes

All these are topics that should be covered in an induction programme when you start a GNVQ. First, you will be introduced to your tutors; usually there will be several for each programme, plus specialist teachers for some of the core skills. Many centres with little experience of running vocational courses will be recruiting suitably qualified teachers rather than expecting existing teachers to adapt their teaching methods to GNVQs.

During the induction period, you will probably carry out a mock GNVQ assignment to give you a flavour of the work involved and enable your tutors to identify your strengths and weaknesses – including any special needs – so that they can draw up an individual action plan to help you achieve your goals. At this stage, if you and your tutors decide that you are not suited to the vocational area or the level you have enrolled for, you will probably be given the opportunity to transfer to another programme.

If you are taking a GNVQ at school, you may be introduced to the qualifications in the academic year before the actual programme begins. At one school, students are briefed on the GNVQ option in November and, if they choose to take it up, they join an induction programme beginning in late June. This consists of an initial two weeks' bridging course, followed by a lengthy run-in to the GNVQ itself that takes up the first half of the autumn term. Parents are encouraged to attend some of the introductory sessions. Some schools also encourage students to visit local businesses during the holidays to find out as much as possible about different occupations before they choose a specific GNVQ.

‘We run a three-week induction programme. When the students arrive, they know which vocational area they're in, but some of them won't know what level they'll be placed at. During the programme, we do some initial evaluation to make sure they're put on the right programme. We do move people between levels. Usually the movement is from Intermediate to Advanced level, but we do have some students moving the other way.

‘We introduce them to Leisure and Tourism and show them what the area is like. They do exercises in team-building and they are given a three-week assignment which has to be handed in on the last day. This teaches them about deadlines and gives them an idea of the requirements of a GNVQ assignment.

‘We organise some theatre visits to London and they also mix with other groups of students. We've got performing arts students at this college and they help the new Leisure and Tourism students develop a circus tricks routine. It's mainly a team-building exercise, but when they've got the act sorted, they put on the show for an audience.

‘At the end of the three weeks, they start the course as prescribed.

A flexible timetable

A GNVQ programme has a less rigid timetable than the courses you have been used to. There are compulsory classroom sessions, workshops and tutorials, but much of your work will be activity-based and self-directed and may involve carrying out projects outside the classroom. To some extent you can work at your own pace, but you must meet deadlines. As a GNVQ tutor emphasised:

> Students must realise that they have to complete work on units by a certain time. They have to stick to the timetable worked out with their teachers, because if they don't, they will find themselves starting work on another unit before they have finished the first one. The knock-on effect means that they risk reaching the end of the programme with few units completed.
>
> 'Here, we monitor the students' progress carefully. Teachers send letters to students asking them to report with finished work by a particular date. We also keep in touch with parents, informing them of their children's progress and explaining the need for GNVQ students to keep up with the programmes.

In practice, a GNVQ programme at the two higher levels should take up around half your weekly learning time – more if it includes several additional units. The awarding bodies recommend that a total of about 60 hours of structured learning should be allowed for each vocational unit, plus additional time to carry out projects. Work on more than one unit may be carried out simultaneously and be spread over several weeks – which makes it all the more important to stick to deadlines.

Activity

At one college, Advanced GNVQ students receive 60 hours of teacher input per unit, and are expected to put in 30 hours of self-directed activity – research, assignments, writing up reports, etc. They spend 18 hours per week in the classroom, the time being allocated equally to three units. Each classroom session lasts two hours and may take the form of a lecture given by a tutor, a talk given by a guest speaker, or an instructional video. During some of these sessions, assignments are planned and reviewed. In addition, there are core skills tutorials or workshops, and students can also attend voluntary classes where they can pick up or refine extra skills.

At some schools and colleges you will be expected to complete work on a group of units by the end of a ten-week term. Other centres divide the GNVQ year into six-month semesters and organise work on groups of units accordingly.

Year two of Advanced GNVQs can offer students the chance to specialise in areas of individual interest. 'In Leisure and Tourism', a tutor explained, 'the students can take a leisure route – concentrating on additional units in leisure travel services, tour operations – or a sports route – perhaps doing sports science or sports coaching.'

IMPORTANT !

➨ Don't expect to work your way through the programme unit by unit, spending a fixed number of hours working on one unit before moving on to the next.

➨ You are more likely to work on a group of several units at once.

To show how wide the range can be, here is a list of the additional units which one college offers its Advanced Leisure and Tourism students:

1. Travel, tourism and geography
2. Leisure travel services
3. Sports and recreation
4. Countryside recreation
5. Health and fitness
6. Arts and entertainment
7. Business travel
8. Tour operations

9. Conference and exhibitions organisation
10. Heritage tourism
11. Third World tourism
12. Conservation
13. Investigating physical recreation
14. Farm tourism
15. Sports science
16. Principles of sports coaching
17. Legal aspects of leisure and tourism
18. Managing the performing arts
19. Equine management
20. Sports psychology.

Whatever their timetabling arrangements, most centres will concentrate on the mandatory units first, followed by the optional units, with any additional units being left until the requirements for a full award have been met.

Work on the core skills units is usually integrated with that of the vocational units, but in certain circumstances may be carried out separately. For example, if students joining Foundation and Intermediate programmes have no computer skills, these may be 'front-loaded' into the first weeks of the programme, so that by the end of the first term the students can apply them to the vocational units.

Vocational units

The vocational units are the backbone of any GNVQ programme. All the activities you undertake will be carried out to meet the requirements of these units, so it pays to look at them in some detail. The basic structure of vocational units is the same whether they are mandatory, optional or additional. Core skills units are rather different, and are dealt with in a separate chapter. Bear in mind, though, that you will be expected to apply core skills in a vocational context – that is, within the activities designed around the vocational units.

Each vocational unit names a particular *area of competence* within the general vocational area. For example, in Unit 3 of the mandatory units of Advanced Leisure and Tourism, the area of competence specified is 'Providing customer service'. In Unit 3 of Intermediate Health and Social Care, the area of competence is 'Health emergencies'.

Units tell you which area of competence you will be working in, but they are basically titles, not instructions. To find out about the kind of evidence you will be expected to produce to prove your competence, you have to break down the unit into its different parts. Let's dismantle Unit 3 from Intermediate Health and Social Care, so that we'll be able to see how the parts relate to the assignments you will be set.

Elements

Each unit is subdivided into smaller parts which specify the basic skills, knowledge and understanding you must achieve in a particular area. These subdivisions are called *elements* and there are between two and five in each unit. In the 'Health emergencies' unit, there are three elements:

- ➤ 3.1 – Identify health emergencies
- ➤ 3.2 – Respond to emergencies
- ➤ 3.3 – Explain health and safety principles relevant to emergencies.

Performance criteria

At first glance, the elements may look horribly vague. In Advanced Business, one element requires candidates to 'Explain government influences on business' – a task that would daunt even the Chancellor of the Exchequeur. Fortunately, the skills and knowledge you must apply are set out in a list of performance criteria, which identify only what you must do in order to meet the requirements of the element.

Basically, '*performance criteria*' is a fancy way of saying '*essential things you must do*'. 'Essential' is the key word. To achieve a particular element, you must meet *all* the performance criteria, though not necessarily on the same occasion.

Sticking with the example from Intermediate Health and Social Care, let's home in on Element 3.2, 'Respond to emergencies'. This element has five performance criteria:

➤ procedures for organising the attendance of emergency services are explained
➤ procedures for assisting injured people until services arrive are explained
➤ own limitations are identified in relation to assisting injured people
➤ materials necessary for the provision of basic first-aid are explained
➤ care procedures are identified and explained in relation to health emergencies.

IMPORTANT!

➤ Look at the verbs in any list of performance criteria. They identify what you are being asked to *do*.

In the performance criteria listed above, you are asked to 'explain' or 'identify' or 'identify and explain'. Performance criteria for other units may ask you to 'describe', 'evaluate', 'select', 'prepare', 'investigate', etc. That sounds simple enough, but GNVQ teachers say that quite a few students don't pay sufficient attention to the verbs. The result is that they may 'identify' instead of 'evaluating', or 'describe' instead of 'investigating'.

Performance criteria are about 'doing', which means that evidence which meets the requirements will come from activities, not just from written reports or descriptions. For example, to meet the performance criteria listed above, you might take part in a simulated emergency – a domestic fire, say. You would have to show that you could organise the attendance of the appropriate emergency services and that you were familiar with basic safety precautions, such as moving people to safety. Obviously, you would be expected to act sensibly, recognising your own limitations in such a situation. You would also have to demonstrate that you were familiar with basic first-aid materials and procedures.

REMEMBER!

•▸ You don't have to meet all the performance criteria at one time.

•▸ The evidence will probably come from several activities carried out over a period of time.

Range

The performance criteria give a pretty clear idea of the essential skills and knowledge you must achieve. But because some of them could cover a very wide range of activities, each element also includes a list of range statements which indicate the depth and breadth of coverage required. They set clear limits around the performance and knowledge you will be expected to demonstrate.

Like the performance criteria, all the range statements must be met. 'There might be eight to ten things in the range,' a student pointed out, 'but though each one might take only a couple of lines in a report, you have to be able to prove that you did it.'

Returning to the element from Intermediate Health and Social Care 'Respond to emergencies', you will see that it has four range statements that indicate the depth and breadth of coverage required:

•▸ **Organising attendance of emergency services**: procedures in the event of accidents; procedures in the event of illness; procedures in care and in public and domestic settings

- **Procedures for assisting injured people:** safety precautions; decisions to assist with movement or not to move people
- **Materials:** contents of first-aid box (eg adhesive dressings, sterile dressings, sterile eye pads, triangular bandages, crepe roll bandages, safety pins)
- **Care procedures:** monitoring of levels of consciousness; resuscitation; identification of skeletal injury; procedures for preventing infection; intake of poisons; absorption of chemical or poisonous substances; dressing wounds; burns/scald treatment.

Activity

One tutor describes *range* as 'different situations in which evidence is demonstrated. For example, on a "Customer care" assignment in Leisure and Tourism, the students had to demonstrate that they could deal with different types of customer – satisfied, dissatisfied, people they knew, people they didn't know – in different circumstances – face to face, on the phone, etc. The students did this through a video where they demonstrated their skills in the range of circumstances they might be expected to come across in that particular area.'

Evidence indicators

Underneath the range statements of an element is another list indicating the general forms in which evidence against the performance criteria and range should be presented. These are the evidence indicators; below are some examples.

For Element 5.2 of Health and Social Care, this section reads:

- **Evidence indicators:** an explanation of emergency care skills, to include procedures for organising the attendance of emergency services, and identification of own limitations in relation to treating injured people.

Written	Visual	Three dimensional	Oral
Report	Display	Models	Performance
Diary	Poetry	Sculpture	Role-play
Log	Map-making	Produce	Recorded discussions
Essay	Storyboard	Artefacts	Recorded conversations
Story	Test paper		Interview
Questionnaire	Photograph		Debate
Letter	Decoration		Presentations
Notes/draft	Graph		Commentaries
Newspaper	Print-out		
	Demonstration		
	Picture		
	Poster		
	Diagram		
	Film		
	Video		

The 'explanation' in this case may take the form of a written report or a discussion or a visual presentation. In many elements, the evidence indicators call for a report or a presentation or a case-study, but depending on the requirements of the element, valid evidence may come in almost any form.

Evidence may be generated by a huge range of activities:

•► writing

•► reading

•► measuring

•► singing

- calculating
- map-reading
- performing
- illustrating
- interviewing

- questioning
- designing
- translating
- surveying, etc.

Projects and assignments

To make sure that your activities generate the evidence that meets the requirements of the elements, they will be organised as formal projects or assignments with specific tasks, goals and deadlines. Besides allowing students to meet the performance criteria, the assignments should:

- allow evidence to emerge
- accommodate students' individual needs and previous experience
- give clear guidance without stifling individual initiative
- integrate core skills where relevant
- be accompanied by documentation for assessment, grading and recording.

In some cases, you may be allowed to devise your own assignments, subject to your tutors' approval. Usually, though, assignments are set by the tutors, who take great pains to design activities that are relevant, interesting and manageable.

'We set two or three major assignments to cover the units in one block,' explained a tutor. 'Then there are lots of peripheral activities, including classroom work, where the students mop up the missing elements.'

===== **Activity** =====

Here, in the words of GNVQ students from the same school, are some examples of assignments carried out in different programmes.

Leisure and Tourism

 We produced a staff guide for a sports centre. It included information on how to dress, how to approach customers and what they would expect of us. We also had to set out disciplinary procedures.

Health and Social Care

 We did a personal social development project. We developed an hour-long lesson on AIDS for 14-year-olds.

Business

 We designed our own board game as if we were manufacturing it for production. We had to work out costs and a marketing strategy. It was done in a group, but each individual had their own role. We received help from Waddingtons, the board game manufacturer.

At one school, an Intermediate Business student used her own initiative to find a part-time junior job at a solicitor's office, where she was able to 'compare structures and functions in business organisations', an element of one of her Business units. At the same school, two Advanced Health and Social Care students decided to tape-record an interview with a hearing-impaired student in order to meet the requirements for an element entitled 'Communicate with individuals'.

Your assignment will be presented in the form of a written brief and will be accompanied by a cover sheet telling you which elements of which units it is designed to cover. Some assignments will cover some or all the requirements of a single element, some will cover different elements of the same unit, and some will cover different elements of different units.

Some assignments will be carried out individually, but more complex activities covering several elements will usually be done in a group or team, with individuals being allocated specific tasks or roles. Some assignments may involve students on other GNVQ programmes. At some centres, Intermediate and Advanced students in the same vocational areas are taught together – at least in the first year. But most schools and colleges deliver the programmes separately.

Individual assignment: an example

Here is an example of an assignment that targets a single element, 'Assess the impact of competition on marketing activity', from Unit 7, 'Marketing', in the 1992–93 Advanced Business programme.

The element has four performance criteria:

1. Effects of competition between suppliers on consumer choice are identified.
2. Effects of consumer demand on suppliers are identified.
3. Effects on marketing activity of supplier attempts to gain the leading edge are identified.
4. Influence of competition on publicity and advertising is assessed.

Either comparing Tesco with Sainsbury's, or Superdrug with Boots, produce an in-depth study of the two suppliers comparing their marketing activities.

You should aim to look at the following factors:

➡ how competition between the two companies affects consumer choice

➡ how consumer demand affects what the companies sell

➡ the marketing and advertising strategies the companies use in an attempt to gain the leading edge

➡ the influence of competition on their publicity and advertising.

Your study should include reference to:

➡ competition aspects like prices, fair trading and monopolies

➡ the effects of competition on product development, customer service and efficiency in the companies

➡ the companies' marketing activities, including corporate image, marketing strategy, price wars and incentives to buy.

You may find that the only way to obtain the information is to contact the companies concerned. Please obtain college permission if you wish to conduct a telephone or personal interview with staff from the companies involved (unless you already have a personal contact). Before permission is given, you will need to show the staff the questions you intend to ask and that you have done as much research as possible from journals, periodicals and newspapers, etc.

Working as a group: 'Managing an event: parents' evening'

The following group assignment, 'Managing an event: parents' evening', was set for college students on the 1992–93 Advanced Leisure and Tourism programme. It was designed to cover three elements of Unit 3, 'Providing customer service', one element of Unit 5, 'Planning for an event', and one element of the additional core skills unit, 'Personal Skills – Working with Others'.

As a group, you are asked to plan, manage and evaluate a

parents' evening for Intermediate and Advanced Leisure and Tourism. The date, time and place for the meeting have already been determined:

- date: Monday 8 February
- time: 6.30–8.30 pm
- venue: Park Room Restaurant, Jubilee House.

You are responsible for managing and monitoring the event and liaising with Intermediate Leisure and Tourism students, who will be carrying out the event in accordance with your instructions and guidance.

IMPORTANT!

- Detailed records should be kept for the group and subgroups throughout. On-going communication is vital, both among yourselves and between your group and all those you will be dealing with: staff, other students, parents, administrative staff, etc.

You will also be expected to evaluate the success of your planning and its implementation.

Initial planning or stage 1
Working in small groups, then double-checking as one large group:

- identify the main factors to consider in organising this event
- note people to contact, and how
- outline initial checklists of equipment, materials and preparation needed by Intermediate students in key areas – eg reception, refreshments, displays.

Follow-on or stage 2

Once you have recognised the extent and constraints of your brief, and know when you can liaise with Intermediate students:

- ➻ appoint a project leader to co-ordinate the work of the groups and liaise with staff as required
- ➻ complete an overall time management plan for the project
- ➻ confirm and review work undertaken in stage 1
- ➻ in your groups, in consultation with the project leader, agree roles and responsibilities and draw up action plans
- ➻ carry out your allocated tasks.

Briefing or stage 3

Your planning will need to be exact, detailed and clear to enable all aspects to be covered and for Intermediate students to receive in good time all the information, schedules and guidance they need to carry out your instructions accurately.

Monitoring of event or stage 4
Run, monitor and evaluate the event.

Recording
Planning sessions for each small group should be run professionally, each group acting as a committee and recording all decisions. The leader or representative from each group should notify the project leader of progress and decisions, and the project leader has the responsibility of ensuring that all groups know what is happening. The project leader may wish to run a full class meeting from time to time to review progress.

REMEMBER !

➻ A copy of all documents produced and received – eg letters, memos, checklists, schedules, rotas, etc – should be filed in the 'parents' evening file' provided. This makes for easy reference for everyone, progress can be readily monitored and any gaps are more likely to be spotted.

Following the event, each group will submit a report detailing its contribution and effectiveness. The project leader will provide an overview of the whole process. You should all include feedback on customer care.

The whole class will be involved in collating and indexing the final report file, making clear each member's contribution.

Assessment
Please note that the assessment criteria for Advanced level are based on two units – Unit 5: 'Planning for an event or function' and Unit 3: 'Providing customer care'.

Unit 3:   3.2 – Plan a customer care programme
              3.3 – Provide customer service
              3.4 – Evaluate the operation of the
                    customer care programme
Unit 5:   5.2 – Present a plan for an event

Core skills: 'Personal Skills – Working with Others': 3.2

Apart from the assessment requirements, this assignment is of course an excellent opportunity to demonstrate practically your customer care skills to a wide range of people. It is worth pausing for a minute to identify exactly who all these customers are – internal and external.

Good luck, and enjoy the assignment!

Work-related assignments

Because GNVQ is a vocational programme, many of your activities will involve out-of-school links with business and industry. These will range from visits to local businesses and talks from experts in particular vocational areas, to actual work placements. The amount of work experience varies from centre to centre, with some schools and colleges organising only the odd day or two and others arranging as much as six weeks. At some centres, the teachers themselves prepare for vocational programmes by going on appropriate work placements.

Most schools and colleges already have strong links with local businesses and have gone to great efforts to develop these even further for GNVQ students. At one school, students were taught for one day per week (equivalent) in school and trained for one day per week in the workplace. Among the partners in this enterprise were: banks; the County Council education, social services and library departments; engineering firms; a large hotel group; a national construction company; and British Nuclear Fuels.

Another school found that the stationery chain W H Smith was prepared to offer students work experience across all the five GNVQs then available, while a local hospital provided opportunities for assignments in Health and Social Care, and also helped in the teaching of one of the units.

Local Training and Enterprise Councils (TECs) may be able to help GNVQ centres find employers who will provide students with the richness of experience that work placement gives. The TECs are closely involved with NVQs, the workplace equivalent of GNVQs, and they have links with many local employers.

Keeping track – documentation

Several projects, carried out over a number of weeks, might be necessary to meet all the requirements for a single unit, so it is vitally important that both students and tutors keep track of progress. This involves a certain amount of paperwork.

The awarding bodies issue log books for recording students' achievements. Colour-coded and designed for easy cross-reference, they tell students and tutors at a glance what has been achieved and what targets have still to be met. Details and layout may vary from centre to centre, but a typical record sheet matches assignments against units. The units are broken down, column by column, into the unit elements, performance criteria and range, and as each target is achieved, the appropriate box is ticked off. Most centres also issue record sheets summarising progress towards achieving groups of units (mandatory vocational, optional vocational, core skills, etc) and the full award.

Some students complain about the volume of paperwork they have to manage:

There's too much paperwork, too much cross-referencing, especially if a project covers more than one unit. There are too many forms to fill in.

But one student said:

 I thought the paperwork was useful. It helps
you keep track of what you've done and
prevents wasting time.

Portfolio of Evidence

All the evidence and relevant documentation generated by
your activities are kept in a Portfolio of Evidence – a sturdy
ring file or similar. You will probably find it useful to keep
two portfolios – one for finished work and one for work in
progress. For ease of reference – not only for yourself, but
also for your assessors and other interested parties – it will
help to organise the material logically and to provide an
index. Indexing your portfolio is one of the tasks you will be
taught during the induction programme. Most GNVQ students become very proud of their portfolio.

Do not cram absolutely everything you produce into
your portfolio. It should contain only the evidence relevant
to the GNVQ units you wish to be assessed in. This will
include:

- ➻ evidence generated through projects or assignments
- ➻ evidence of underpinning knowledge and
  understanding. This may come from oral or written
  questioning or tests or other school or college
  activities
- ➻ evidence from other sources provided that it can be
  authenticated and is clearly relevant (eg a report by an
  employer, or a certificate or prize)
- ➻ evidence of unit test performance
- ➻ records of assessor decisions.

Activity

That sounds a lot and, as a tutor in Leisure and Tourism
explained, some students are a bit daunted at the prospect.

❦ The students immediately think of a whole year's work, all written, and some of them get frightened. But it's not like that. The evidence may be made up of an observed role-play, a practical demonstration or a display such as an advertisement or poster. At this college we have a mock reception area where the students telephone each other on business calls, make and take bookings, and deal with customer complaints and enquiries. We tape or video these exchanges and then play the recording back to the group, discuss their performance, point out mistakes and get feedback. At the end, what they put in their portfolios is a piece of paper that simply records what they did and whether their performance met the criteria. That doesn't fit in with the picture of a portfolio. ❜

Assessment

Individual work

At frequent intervals – after you have completed assignments, for example – the evidence you have collected will be assessed to see if it covers all the requirements for an element or unit. The assessment process starts with you. You have the responsibility not only for collecting the evidence, but also for storing and presenting it in a way that is readily accessible to the assessors. Hence the need to index your portfolio.

Assessment is carried out internally, by your programme tutors, who will be looking for evidence of what you have achieved, not how you achieved it, nor how long it took.

If the assessors judge that you have presented sufficient evidence to meet all the requirements for, say, a unit (all the elements, all the performance criteria and all the range statements), you will have achieved that particular unit. The achievement will be credited and you can move on to another part of your programme. If the assessors decide that evidence is lacking, you will be told where it falls short and will be given guidance on how to make up the missing evidence.

Group activities

Assessing individual work is relatively straightforward, but group projects or assignments may cause problems. The following cautionary tale was told by a tutor who asked her Leisure and Tourism students to organise and evaluate a charity event for a student who had fallen ill.

Each member had a different role – ordering the food, fixing the venue, publicising the event – with one member supervising the whole project. Unfortunately, that person didn't co-ordinate the work properly, so we had to review the project again, impose a deadline and order of working. The event went well. We raised quite a lot of money. Then came the time for assessment. In addition to their individual roles, each group member had been told that they must give their own evaluation of the event. But only one person produced an evaluation, so the whole piece of work was referred [failed]. The students were told that nobody passed until the evaluation was done properly. After that there was a flurry of activity, but the students struggled because they didn't trust the original group leader and no one wanted to take on the responsibility. The whole thing went round and round for a couple of weeks, and then we had a showdown. A firm deadline was given, and finally the evaluations appeared.

'Some members who had played their part well were very annoyed, but they had been told that the work would be assessed as a *group* enterprise. After all, that's how it is in the world of work. If you're all pulling in different directions, the business loses.

Authenticity of evidence

The assessor will also want to be satisfied that you are genuinely responsible for the evidence presented. In group activities, a tutor pointed out, 'there is a tendency among some individuals to let the more enthusiastic students carry the main responsibilities, and then claim credit for the outcome. But because the work is assessed as a whole and everyone gets the same grade, the ones who did the real work have a go at the shirkers. Peer pressure is the most powerful disincentive to cheat.'

Another tutor suggested that the best way to avoid such problems arising was to allocate specific tasks to individual students. 'At the beginning of each assignment,' he explained, 'the students write down what their individual contribution will be. If a piece of work doesn't come in, we go to the student concerned and say: "You were responsible for that and you haven't done it."'

Assessing to a national standard

First and foremost, your work will be assessed to see if it meets the relevant performance criteria and range statements. These are the *standards* which apply to all GNVQ students, and to make sure that these standards are interpreted correctly and consistently, assessments are checked by verifiers.

There are two kinds of verifier – internal and external. Internal verifiers are staff members of GNVQ centres, while external verifiers are appointed by the awarding bodies.

- ☛ *Internal verifiers* will have the qualifications or experience to judge whether the assessments in a vocational area are accurate. They may be part of a GNVQ programme team, but they can't assess work from their own programmes.
- ☛ *External verifiers* act on behalf of the awarding bodies and visit GNVQ centres regularly to check that suitable procedures are in place and that the standards are being interpreted correctly. The

feedback they provide helps draw the awarding bodies' attention to any problems.

A tutor explains how the process works:

> At the end of an assignment, the programme team will make their assessments, which are then considered by an internal verifier – a member of staff who looks at the assessment decisions from an impartial perspective. The internal verifier checks the assessment against the student's portfolio and decides if it's fair. Then the external verifier comes in. Usually, they don't look at the work itself. Their job is to see if the proper assessment processes are in place and are being implemented correctly. Basically, they're quality controllers.

What happens if you disagree with an assessment decision?

One of the tasks of the internal verifier is to ensure that an appeals procedure is in place and that students have access to it. Each centre will have its own appeals procedure, which should be explained to you during your induction programme.

Unit end tests

Right at the end of the specifications (ie the precise require-ments) for each element of the mandatory vocational units, you will see the statement:

> 'The unit test will confirm the candidate's coverage of range.'

Don't be misled by the small print. The tests are *important*. They are designed to confirm your underlying knowledge and understanding for each of the mandatory vocational units, and in order to achieve a full GNVQ award, you must pass *all* of them.

Mandatory vocational units are the only parts of the GNVQ programme that are always externally tested.

Optional or additional units may be tested internally by the centre, in which case they will be verified or checked by the awarding body to ensure that standards are being met. There are no formal tests for core skills units. Work on these units is integrated into your projects and assessed accordingly.

The tests follow the same form – short-answer or multiple-choice questions lasting an hour and including about 40 items. Because the awarding bodies consider that the knowledge on which the tests are set is essential, the pass mark is high – around 70 per cent. But should you fail the first time, you will be given several opportunities to retake the test for any unit.

You may take the first unit end tests at the end of the first term, having completed work on a block of units. The tests are set for specific dates, but there will be four opportunities to take any one test.

Some views on testing
The subject of tests arouses a lot of argument – among teachers and awarding bodies, as well as students. Many people believe that written tests shouldn't play such an important part in a qualification which is activity-based. There is concern that the tests will come to dominate the programmes, with the assignments being seen as mere preparation for the written papers.

On the whole, though, students seem to have taken the tests in their stride. Here are some comments from a group of students at the same school:

Tests are a good thing. Although you do a lot of work for your assignments, you don't always take in the underlying principles. But if you know you've got tests, you have to think about everything you do.

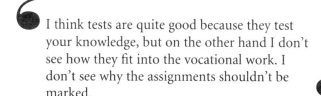

I think tests are quite good because they test your knowledge, but on the other hand I don't see how they fit into the vocational work. I don't see why the assignments shouldn't be marked.

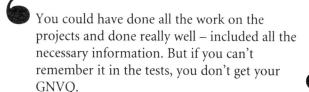

You could have done all the work on the projects and done really well – included all the necessary information. But if you can't remember it in the tests, you don't get your GNVQ.

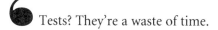

Tests? They're a waste of time.

You might be surprised to learn that you won't be given a mark for the tests. If you pass, you know that you scored 70 per cent or better, and if you get within ten per cent of the pass mark, you will be told. If you get lower than 60 per cent, you will be told that you have failed, but not by how much.

'This makes it difficult to guide or coach the students who don't pass the test,' said one tutor. 'The most you can deduce is that, if a student got within ten per cent of the mark in a test containing 14 questions, they probably failed on one more question than someone who passed with 70 per cent.'

A final comment on tests. The awarding bodies' experience is that students who had difficulty with the tests also had difficulty getting the evidence for their vocational projects.

Certification
When you achieve all the required units in a GNVQ programme and pass the end tests for all the mandatory

vocational units, you automatically gain a Pass. You then receive a certificate listing the titles of the units you have achieved. A certificate listing only one or two units does not necessarily mean that the student has failed to achieve others. Some students will choose to take only certain units, perhaps in addition to GCE A-levels or other qualifications.

IMPORTANT!

➻ At the time of writing, no additional units have been approved by the NCVQ. Until they are, they will not be credited on your GNVQ certificate, but will be recorded on a separate record of achievement issued by the awarding body.

Grading

GNVQs are awarded at three grades – Pass, Merit and Distinction. If you have achieved a Pass, your work will be assessed for the grades of Merit and Distinction. The assessment is based solely on the work presented in your Portfolio of Evidence. Neither unit tests nor additional units count for grading purposes. Individual units are not graded separately.

For grading purposes, the assessors are mainly interested in the process rather than the product – the skills you used to achieve the outcomes to your assignments, not the outcomes themselves. In general terms, they will be assessing your capacity to manage your own learning. Specifically, they will be looking for evidence of your skills in:

➻ planning
➻ information seeking and information handling
➻ evaluation.

The fourth grading criterion is:

●→ quality of outcomes.

To grade this, assessors look at your work and decide how far its quality reflects your ability to bring together the knowledge, skills and understanding relevant to the area you are working in. They also assess how well you use the 'language' of your GNVQ area. By this they mean the standard forms of communication within your area, including the ideas and concepts conveyed by any specialist vocabulary.

When deciding whether to award a Merit or a Distinction, the assessors use certain criteria to measure how these skills have been applied. Basically, they will consider whether you have applied the skills, independently or with guidance, to straightforward tasks or to complex activities.

A Merit grade will be awarded if your work consistently demonstrates that you can apply these skills to straightforward tasks, with guidance if necessary. A straightforward task might be a single-stage task, such as conducting an interview with someone you know. You probably wouldn't need to do much planning to set up the interview, and opportunities to use information seeking and evaluation skills would probably be limited. To give you a Merit for quality of outcomes, assessors would be looking at a discrete task you had completed. They would assess whether you are effective in the language of your GNVQ area.

A *Distinction grade* will be awarded if your work consistently demonstrates that you can apply these skills to complex activities, without guidance. A complex activity, such as a market survey, might include a series of stages. You would need to plan a course of action by organising tasks in order of priority and by deciding how best to gather and process (handle) the information you require. Finally, you would be expected to evaluate the results of the survey. When grading you for Distinction on quality of outcomes, assessors would be looking at a complex task you had completed. You would need to be fluent in the 'language' of your GNVQ area.

Consistency of grading evidence

To achieve a grade of Merit or Distinction, at least one-third of the work in your portfolio should demonstrate that you have applied the relevant skills to your activities. The assessor will be looking for consistency of evidence, so will review your work as a whole, not just look at one chunk. In fact, the assessor will also be looking to see that you have developed skills in the course of your programme, which means that you shouldn't be too worried if your earlier work is not worthy of the higher grades.

It is likely that most of your best work will be done towards the end of the programme. 'We don't expect students to produce brilliant work at the start of the programme,' said one GNVQ tutor. 'If they did, there would be little point in their doing the course.'

Grading during your programme

Final grading decisions are based on your work as a whole and are made only when you have achieved all the units for

your GNVQ. However, from the start of your GNVQ programme, your tutors will tell you if they think your individual projects are worthy of a Merit or Distinction grade.
These are not final grading decisions. Their main purpose is
to give you an idea of whether you have satisfied the grading
criteria and to make you more aware of how and where you
can improve your skills in planning, information seeking
and handling, and evaluation.

An Advanced Health and Social Care student described
her experience of the grading system:

> It was explained during our induction, but to be
> honest it didn't mean much to me until I'd finished
> the first unit. In fact, that turned out to be the most
> difficult unit because I had to do so much of the work on
> my own. My tutor told me that the unit was of Distinction
> standard and encouraged me to go for the highest grade for
> the whole programme. That meant I did as much work as
> possible on my own, using my initiative. By the end of the
> programme, though, I was running out of time and had to
> do two units in two weeks. Obviously, they're not up to
> Distinction standard, but I should get a pass for them. I'm
> hoping that enough of the rest of my work is good
> enough to get me a Distinction.

Another student explained how GNVQ students can con-
tribute to the grading process and use feedback from their
assessors to improve their performance:

> After finishing a project I sit down with my tutor and
> discuss the work. I tell her what standard I think I've
> achieved before she assesses it. Several times I've thought I
> deserved a Merit or a Distinction, but the assessor gave me
> only a Pass. That wasn't the end of the world, though,
> because I had the chance to go over the work again. In fact,

now that I've finished the programme, I'm going through my whole portfolio again, trying to bring it up to Distinction standard – or at least Merit. If I'm not sure about a piece of work, I can show it to the assessor, and if she doesn't think it's good enough, I'll take it away and improve it.

IMPORTANT!

➻ You can try to improve your grade, but don't expect to be able to redo an entire project from scratch. You won't have time and will risk falling behind on other units.

Activity

The grading process actually starts with the students themselves. This is how it works at one college:

We put students into a position where they have to do their own grading. For each assignment they are given an Assignment Planner, which is a sheet with questions that the students must answer in the appropriate boxes. The students have to ask themselves: "What do I need to know? What do I need to do? In which order? By when? Have I achieved it? If not, why not? What do I need to do next? How successful was what I have done?"

'The first four questions involve planning, so if they fill in those boxes – with advice from their tutor, if necessary – they have fulfilled the planning element. If they then cover "Have I achieved what I was doing? If not, why not?

What do I need to know next?" then they've done their evaluation. We make them do planning and evaluation for every assignment.

At one school, the assignment briefs come with three sheets – one for planning and one for evaluation, plus a grading log. On the planning sheet are five boxes that have to be filled in by the student. These are headed:

- Plan of action
- What information will be needed?
- Where will it come from?
- How will your evidence be presented?

On the evaluation sheet, the following information is requested:

- What did I achieve?
- What did I learn?
- What would I change and why?
- Record of teacher/tutor intervention
- Recommendations.

The grading log sets out the grading themes with boxes in which the student can summarise evidence against the grading criteria for Merit or Distinction. (Now you understand why GNVQ students complain about too much paperwork.)

There is no separate sheet for recording information skills because these emerge from the actual work presented as evidence in the portfolio.

Support systems

Inevitably, there will be times when an assignment doesn't work out as planned. What happens then?

If practicable, you will do it again, but if it was a complex group assignment that can't easily be repeated, you might have to pick up the missing evidence from a different assignment. In no circumstances would you not be given the opportunity to achieve the missing requirements. At one school, the summer holidays arrived and, as an Intermediate GNVQ student said, 'we still had whacking big holes in the evidence. So our teacher set projects to help fill the gaps, and we finished the work in our holidays.'

There is little chance of your falling behind without your tutors noticing. The assessment process and individual review procedures are designed to keep you and your tutors informed of your progress and to prepare appropriate plans of action. One school stressed the need for such provision: 'All staff involved in GNVQ and all students studying for a GNVQ fully appreciate the need for, and value of, individual action planning. Students sit down with their programme assessors/teachers and address the questions:

➡ Where are we now?
➡ Where are we going?
➡ How is this assignment going?
➡ How can my next assignment be better?
➡ What might I need to do to be working at merit/ distinction level?
➡ Which core skills elements must I look to, to provide evidence for my next assignment?

'In addition, the centre co-ordinator interviews each GNVQ student for 15 minutes every term to review general progress. Assessment of assignment work, feedback on that assessment and the unit test results provide additional means of monitoring progress.'

A tutor in Leisure and Tourism explained how students could be helped. 'If we see someone falling behind, we build something into their programme to help them. If they are a borderline case, we review their work, encourage them to address the areas where they are weak and set extra work in these areas. If they have a particular learning difficulty, such as dyslexia, we get specialist help. But we have to keep an eye out for such problems, because students often try to hide them.'

Another GNVQ teacher who gave tutorials in the numeracy core skill confirmed the reluctance of students to ask for help. 'At each of my core skills tutorials, I ask each student individually if they are having problems. Months after the programme started, the parents of one of the students came to see me. They were annoyed because their daughter was finding numeracy difficult and was receiving no help. I was astounded. She'd been worrying about it for months, and she hadn't said a word to me.'

☞ The message is clear. GNVQ programmes are designed to foster self-reliance, but if you run into problems, don't hesitate to ask for help.

2 Outline of GNVQ Areas and Vocational Units

Refer to this chapter to find out more about:

➨ the vocational area covered by each GNVQ currently available

➨ the vocational units in each GNVQ.

The mandatory units for each GNVQ are the same, regardless of which awarding body or centre is offering the programme. At Foundation level, the optional units are common to all awarding bodies. At Intermediate and Advanced levels, the optional and additional units are set by the individual awarding bodies. The range is so large and varies so widely from centre to centre that it is not practicable to list them here.

For more specific information about the optional and additional units for GNVQs that are available to you, contact your local GNVQ centre.

At Foundation level only, you can choose your optional units from the other vocational units offered by your centre. This allows you to sample different occupational areas before you commit yourself to a particular area at a higher and more demanding level. If you are doing Foundation Manufacturing, for example, you can choose all three of your optional units from this vocational area, or select one or more optional units from Engineering or other vocational areas.

The only restrictions on choice are:

➨ Unit 3 – 'Investigating working in ...'. You can do no more than two of these units in different areas

➨ units which are offered in more than one vocational area are marked '*'. You are allowed to take only one version of these common units.

Art and Design

Art and Design GNVQs give you the opportunity to develop visual language in ways that not only stimulate ideas, but also help you realise them. The qualifications cover art and design, so you will carry out work in both 'art contexts' and 'design contexts'.

- *Art contexts* refer to personal creative activity, where the intention is to produce a response in the viewer or audience.
- *Design contexts* refer to creative activities designed to meet specific needs, such as those required by a client or customer, and therefore they may reflect considerations of functionality, cost, resources and aesthetics.

At Intermediate level you will explore aspects of visual language, present art and design work, develop specific ideas and designs, and investigate business practice in art and design.

At Advanced level you will explore the full range of two-dimensional and three-dimensional visual language, investigate the potential of technology, plan and research art projects, work to design briefs and analyse art and design themes in their historical context – from medieval religion to television and ghetto culture.

Foundation Art and Design

Mandatory units

1. Exploring 2-D art and design techniques
2. Exploring 3-D art and design techniques
3. Investigating working in art and design

Optional units

You will need to complete three units from a range of six, which are common to all awarding bodies:

4.* Contributing to a team activity
5.* Exploring service to customers
6. Promotion and display
7. Designing a product
8. Carrying out an art project
9. Investigating art and design in other vocational areas

Core skills units

1. Application of Number
2. Communication
3. Information Technology

Intermediate Art and Design

Mandatory units

1. Visual language and presentation
2. Explore others' art and design work
3. Develop practical art and design skills
4. Investigate art and design professional practice

Optional units

You will need to complete two optional units from a range of four. Each awarding body offers its own optional units.

Core skills units

1. Application of Number
2. Communication
3. Information Technology

Advanced Art and Design

Mandatory units

1. Two-dimensional visual language
2. Three-dimensional visual language

3. Work with technology
4. Historical and contextual references
5. Business and professional practice
6. Work to art briefs
7. Work to design briefs
8. Evaluate and present work

Optional units

You will need to complete four optional units from a range of about eight. Each awarding body offers its own optional units.

Core skills units

1. Application of Number
2. Communication
3. Information Technology

Business

Business GNVQs offer students the opportunity to develop the skills, knowledge and understanding relevant to any type of business. Since innovation and problem-solving are valuable skills in business, these GNVQs develop creative and analytical thinking through investigating, 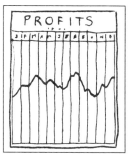 predicting and planning. You will also be encouraged to be imaginative in the way you gather your evidence. You might, for example, set up a business enterprise or undertake work experience, work shadowing and business–education partnerships.

At Intermediate level you will learn about different types of business, their products and employment, the roles of people within business organisations, financial transactions, consumer demand, promoting goods and services, and providing customer care.

At Advanced level you will learn about the economy in which businesses operate, systems for administration and financial accountability, human resourcing, marketing and business planning.

Foundation Business

Mandatory units

1. Processing business payments
2. Investigating business and customers
3. Investigating working in business

Optional units

You will need to complete three optional units from a range of six, which are common to all awarding bodies.

4.* Contributing to a team activity
5.* Health and safety
6.* Scheduling and booking
7. Processing business information
8. Providing office support
9. Investigating employment

Core skills units

1. Application of Number
2. Communication
3. Information Technology

Intermediate Business

Mandatory units

1. Business organisations and employment
2. People in business organisations
3. Financial transactions
4. Consumers and customers

Optional units

You will need to complete two optional units from a range of four. Each awarding body offers its own optional units.

Core skills units

1. Application of Number
2. Communication
3. Information Technology

Advanced Business

Mandatory units

1. Business in the economy
2. Business systems
3. Marketing
4. Human resources
5. Employment in the market economy
6. Financial transactions and monitoring
7. Financial resources
8. Business planning

Optional units

You will need to complete four units from a range of about eight. Each awarding body offers its own optional units.

Core skills units

1. Application of Number
2. Communication
3. Information Technology

Construction and the Built Environment

This GNVQ will be of interest to students planning a career in the construction industry or related areas. The mandatory units at Intermediate level explore the relationship between the built and natural environments, investigate the materials and structural elements of buildings, and explore key operations in the construction industry.

At Advanced level you will explore in greater depth design specifications, properties of construction materials and the technology involved in construction. You will develop knowledge of measurement and costing techniques and investigate the basic skills required to carry out a site investigation and a land survey.

Foundation Construction and the Built Environment

Mandatory units

1. Exploring the natural and built environments
2. Exploring buildings, their use and location
3. Investigating working in the built environment

Optional units

You will need to complete three optional units from a range of six, which are common to all awarding bodies.

4.* Contributing to a team activity
5. Investigating construction craft practices
6. Investigating drawing activities
7.* Health and safety
8. Exploring city communities and new towns
9. The science of buildings

Core skills units

1. Application of Number
2. Communication
3. Information Technology

Intermediate Construction and the Built Environment

Mandatory units

1. Built environment and the community

2. The science of materials and their applications
3. Construction technology and design
4. Construction operations

Optional units

You will need to complete two optional units from a range of four. Each awarding body offers its own optional units.

Core skills units

1. Application of Number
2. Communication
3. Information Technology

Advanced Construction and the Built Environment

Mandatory units

1. Built environment and the community
2. Design, detailing and specification
3. The science of materials and their application
4. Construction and civil engineering technology
5. Construction technology and services
6. Resource management
7. Financing the built environment
8. Surveying processes

Optional units

You will need to complete four optional units from a range of about eight. Each awarding body offers its own optional units.

Core skills units

1. Application of Number
2. Communication
3. Information Technology

Distribution

More than five million people are employed in distribution, warehousing and retail operations, carrying out various functions such as purchasing, marketing, selling and management. Distribution GNVQs provide a broad background to the wide range of activities within this area. They will help you gain experience of  different occupations within each operation, and help you to choose the correct area for further training.

Intermediate Distribution

Mandatory units

1. Distribution, transport and storage
2. Quality and service to the customer
3. Retailing and sales
4. Administration and finance

Optional units

You will need to complete two optional units from a range of four. Each awarding body offers its own optional units.

Core skills units

1. Application of Number
2. Communication
3. Information Technology

Advanced Distribution

Mandatory units

1. Transport and storage
2. Quality and customer service
3. Marketing and sales
4. Purchasing and stock control

5. Finance and administration
6. Responsibilities of managers
7. Human resourcing
8. International trade and distribution

Optional units

You will need to complete four optional units from a range of about eight. Each awarding body offers its own optional units.

Core skills units

1. Application of Number
2. Communication
3. Information Technology

Engineering

Engineering GNVQs are designed to provide opportunities for students to develop the skills, knowledge and understanding that underpin the creation of engineered products, and engineering systems and services. They also provide opportunities to address wider issues regarding the value of engineering to society and the environment.

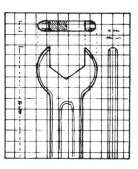

Foundation Engineering

Mandatory units

1. Designing engineered products
2. Making engineered products
3. Investigating working in engineering

Optional units

4. Contributing to a team activity
5. Exploring maths/science through engineered products

6. Application of computers in engineering
7. Servicing and repairing engineered products
8. Introduction to automation in engineering
9. Health and safety

IMPORTANT!

➻ Students intending to progress to GNVQ Engineering at Intermediate level are recommended to choose Unit 5.

Core skills units

1. Application of Number
2. Communication
3. Information Technology

Intermediate Engineering

Mandatory units

1. Engineering materials and processes
2. Graphical communication in engineering
3. Science and mathematics for engineering
4. Engineering in society and the environment

Optional units

You will need to complete two optional units from a range of four. Each awarding body offers its own optional units.

IMPORTANT!

➻ Students intending to progress to Advanced GNVQ in Engineering are strongly recommended to select mathematics (Intermediate) as one of their optional units.

Core skills units

1. Application of Number
2. Communication
3. Information Technology

Advanced Engineering

Mandatory units

1. Engineering and commercial functions in business
2. Engineering systems
3. Engineering processes
4. Engineering materials
5. Design development
6. Engineering in society and the environment
7. Science for engineering
8. Mathematics for engineering

Optional units

You will need to complete four optional units from a range of about eight. Each awarding body offers its own optional units.

> **IMPORTANT!**
>
> - Students intending to progress to higher education are strongly recommended to select mathematics (Advanced) as one of their optional units.

Core skills units

1. Application of Number
2. Communication
3. Information Technology

Health and Social Care

These GNVQs have been designed to allow students an opportunity to develop skills and abilities in the health and social care sectors. The contexts covered by the units include hospitals and community health settings, home care, day care, residential care and early education. The client groups cov-  ered are people of all ages, people with disabilities and people with learning difficulties.

At Intermediate level you will develop the interpersonal skills needed for care work, and investigate the role and function of the health and social care services.

At Advanced level you will explore the central values of caring and investigate the structure of different health and social care services. Your programme will help you to develop knowledge of physical health and health promotion issues, and will provide an introduction to individual care planning and relevant research work.

Foundation Health and Social Care

Mandatory units

1. Understanding health and well-being
2. Understanding personal development and relationships
3. Investigating working in health and social care

Optional units

You will need to complete three units from a range of six, which are common to all the awarding bodies.

4.* Contributing to a team activity
5. Investigating common health emergencies

6. Planning diets
7.* Exploring health and recreational activities
8. Exploring physical care
9. Investigating health and care service provision

Core skills units

1. Application of Number
2. Communication
3. Information Technology

Intermediate Health and Social Care

Mandatory units

1. Provide emotional support
2. Influences on health and well-being
3. Health emergencies
4. Health and social care services

Optional units
You will need to complete two optional units from a range of four. Each awarding body offers its own optional units.

Core skills units

1. Application of Number
2. Communication
3. Information Technology

Advanced Health and Social Care

Mandatory units

1. Access, equal opportunities and client rights
2. Interpersonal interaction
3. Physical aspects of health
4. Psychological and social aspects of health and social care
5. Health promotion
6. Structure and practices in health and social care

7. Care plans
8. Research in health and social care

Optional units

You will need to complete four optional units from a range of about eight. Each awarding body offers its own optional units.

Core skills units

1. Application of Number
2. Communication
3. Information Technology

Hospitality and Catering

These GNVQs develop the customer care skills used in a very wide range of establishments – from fast-food restaurants and luxury hotels to prison canteens and hospitals. Your programme at Intermediate level will give you a grounding in food preparation and provision, accommodation  services and reception. At Advanced level you will look more closely at the commercial aspects of the industry. You will learn about purchasing, costing and finance; investigate the regulations affecting accommodation services; and plan care programmes for a range of customers.

Foundation Hospitality and Catering

Mandatory units

1. Exploring food and drink preparation and service
2. Exploring accommodation operations
3. Investigating working in hospitality and catering

Optional units

You will need to complete three units from a range of six, which are common to all the awarding bodies.

4.* Contributing to a team activity
5. Investigating front-office operations and accommodation services
6.* Planning diets
7. Health, safety and hygiene in hospitality and catering
8. Purchasing, costing and control in hospitality and catering
9. Providing service to customers in hospitality and catering

Core skills units

1. Application of Number
2. Communication
3. Information Technology

Intermediate Hospitality and Catering

Mandatory units

1. Investigating hospitality and catering
2. Customer service in hospitality and catering
3. Providing front-office and accommodation operations
4. Providing food and drink

Optional units

You will need to complete two optional units from a range of four. Each awarding body offers its own optional units.

Core skills units

1. Application of Number
2. Communication
3. Information Technology

Advanced Hospitality and Catering

Mandatory units

1. Investigate the hospitality and catering industry
2. Human resources
3. Provide customer service in hospitality and catering
4. Food preparation and cooking
5. Food and drink service
6. Purchasing, costing and finance
7. Accommodation operations
8. Reception and front-office operations in hospitality

Optional units

You will need to complete four optional units from a range of about eight. Each awarding body offers its own optional units.

Core skills units

1. Application of Number
2. Communication
3. Information Technology

Information Technology

GNVQs in Information Technology provide appropriate qualifications for students who wish to pursue a career in an aspect of information technology, or for those who feel that an understanding of the subject will allow them to study and work more effectively in the future.

At Intermediate level you will investigate the use of information technology in organisations, and its effects on people and society. You will create a simple information-processing system to meet user needs, and you will develop skills in using information technology applications for producing text and graphics and for designing databases.

At Advanced level your investigations will cover data-handling, measurement and control systems, computer modelling, data communications between computer systems, and information technology software. You will also develop skills in systems analysis.

Foundation Information Technology

Mandatory units

1. Using information technology
2. The use and impact of information technology systems
3. Investigating working in information technology

Optional units

You will need to complete three units from a range of six, which are common to all the awarding bodies.

4.* Contributing to a team activity
5. Document production
6. Graphic design
7. Measurement and control systems
8. Obtaining information from electronic sources
9. Information collection and processing

Core skills units

1. Application of Number
2. Communication
3. Information Technology

Intermediate Information Technology

Mandatory units

1. Organisations and the application of information technology

2. People and information technology
3. Developing information-processing systems
4. Using information technology

Optional units

You will need to complete a total of two optional units from a range of four. Each awarding body offers its own optional units.

Core skills units

1. Application of Number
2. Communication
3. Information Technology

Advanced Information Technology

Mandatory units

1. Data handling
2. Measurement and control systems and modelling
3. Communications and networking
4. Software, software installation and software customisation
5. Systems analysis
6. Data modelling and database structures
7. Individuals, society and information technology
8. Information technology projects and teamwork

Optional units

You will need to complete four optional units from a range of about eight. Each awarding body offers its own optional units.

Core skills units

1. Application of Number
2. Communication
3. Information Technology

Leisure and Tourism

The Leisure and Tourism GNVQs provide opportunities for you to demonstrate your command of the essential skills, knowledge and understanding required across the whole range of leisure and tourism industries.

Intermediate level focuses on the local leisure and tourism industry. You will investigate the products, services and employment opportunities associated with local facilities – hotels, gyms, travel agencies, etc. You will actively undertake roles in customer service and promoting products and services, as well as the planning delivery and evaluation of a real event or service. You will also carry out research to ensure that you are familiar with conditions and practices in different leisure and tourism facilities and understand the needs and expectations of customers.

At Advanced level you will investigate the leisure and tourism industries across the UK. Your programme will provide practical coverage of such topics as teamwork, customer service and health and safety. Other units focus on marketing, planning for events, management information and evaluation of the performance of leisure and tourism facilities.

Foundation Leisure and Tourism

Mandatory units

1. Providing service to customers
2. Preparing visitor information materials
3. Investigating working in leisure and tourism

Optional units

You will need to complete three optional units out of the six, which are common to all the awarding bodies.

4.* Contributing to a team activity
5. Presentation and display
6.* Scheduling and booking
7. Exploring leisure travel and tourism
8.* Exploring health and recreational activities
9. Receiving payments

Core skills units

1. Application of Number
2. Communication
3. Information Technology

Intermediate Leisure and Tourism

Mandatory units

1. Investigating leisure and tourism
2. Contributing to an event or service
3. Customer service
4. Promoting products and services

Optional units

You will need to complete two optional units from a range of four. Each awarding body offers its own optional units.

Core skills units

1. Application of Number
2. Communication
3. Information Technology

Advanced Leisure and Tourism

Mandatory units

1. Investigating the leisure and tourism industry
2. Maintaining health, safety and security

3. Providing customer service
4. Marketing in leisure and tourism
5. Planning for an event
6. Providing management information services
7. Working in teams
8. Evaluating the performance of facilities

Optional units

You will need to complete four optional units from a range of about eight. Each awarding body offers its own optional units.

Core skills units

1. Application of Number
2. Communication
3. Information Technology

Management Studies

The Management Studies GNVQ is offered at Advanced level only to students interested in becoming managers. It also provides a path for those wishing to progress to further management qualifications, a variety of other employment opportunities, and to NVQs or higher education. Preferably, you should have some work  experience. Little or no managerial experience should not be an obstacle to entering the course.

In Advanced Management Studies your programme will focus on:

●▶ the roles, responsibilities and working demands made on managers
●▶ how managers function within any commercial, service or industrial environment in the private, public or voluntary sectors

➡ aspects of the operation of organisations and their different functions

➡ how managers mediate the achievement of organisational goals.

Advanced Management Studies

Mandatory units

1. Managers' responsibilities
2. Organisations and managers' roles
3. Services and products
4. Customer relationships
5. Interpersonal communication
6. Employment, recruitment and development
7. Budgets and accounts
8. Handling information

Optional units

You will need to complete four optional units from a range of about eight. Each awarding body offers its own optional units.

Core skills units

1. Application of Number
2. Communication
3. Information Technology

Manufacturing

Manufacturing GNVQs provide opportunities for you to develop the skills, knowledge and under-standing that underpin the main manufacturing functions. The qualification is forward-looking and based on the needs of modern industry regardless of the types of product manufactured. You will

not be expected to cover all aspects of the manufacturing sectors, but you will be asked to demonstrate your understanding of the principles and skills relevant to all areas of manufacturing. You can take advantage of local opportunities in specific industries, although you may not specialise in a single material or product. In many cases, you will need to provide evidence for two contrasting types of product and scales of production. The key terms are:

☞ Materials: Food; textiles/fabric; constructional (wood, metal, plastics, ceramics); electrical/electronic; chemical/biological

☞ Products: Food/drink; textile; durable; paper and board; electrical/electronic; chemical/biological

☞ Scale of production: Continuous; repetitive batch; small batch; single item (eg prototype)

The mandatory units at Intermediate level develop an understanding of producing designs, production planning, process operations and quality, safety and the environment.

At Advanced level you will develop an understanding of manufacturing systems, designing products to meet customer requirements, production costs and schedules, and manufacturing processes. The mandatory units also emphasise the importance of quality assurance and control, health and safety, working in teams, and the impact of manufacturing on the environment.

Foundation Manufacturing

Mandatory units

1. Manufacturing products
2. Exploring manufacturing operations
3. Investigating working in manufacturing

Optional units

You will need to complete three optional units out of the six, which are common to all the awarding bodies.

4.* Contributing to a team activity
5.* Exploring service to customers
6.* Health and safety
7. Making a product
8. Investigating the environmental impact of manufacturing operations
9. Maintaining quality of products

Core skills units

1. Application of Number
2. Communication
3. Information Technology

Intermediate Manufacturing

Mandatory units

1. Working with a design specification
2. Production plan
3. Process operations
4. Quality, safety and the environment

Optional units

You will need to complete two optional units from a range of four. Each awarding body offers its own optional units.

Core skills units

1. Application of Number
2. Communication
3. Information Technology

Advanced Manufacturing

Mandatory units

1. Design specification

2. Communicate product design
3. Manufacturing systems
4. Production costs and schedules
5. Process operations
6. Quality and control
7. Work practices
8. Environmental impact

Optional units

You will need to complete four optional units from a range of about eight. Each awarding body offers its own optional units.

Core skills units

1. Application of Number
2. Communication
3. Information Technology

Media: Communication and Production

Media GNVQs develop the skills and understanding that underpin the creation and production of individual media items and finished media products. At Intermediate level you will learn, for example, how to plan and produce an audio-visual product (eg a video or radio programme), and investigate media texts and audiences.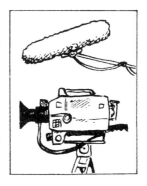

At Advanced level you will develop further your knowledge, skills and understanding of the subject in producing, for instance, a wider range of material and investigating in more detail the media industries, languages and genres.

Intermediate Media

Mandatory units

1. Investigating media products and audiences
2. Planning and producing a print and graphics product
3. Planning and producing an audio-visual product
4. Investigating local, regional and national media

Optional units

5. Making sense of the media
6. Creating material for media products
7. Creating a narrative
8. Making a media product

Core skills units

1. Application of Number
2. Communication
3. Information Technology

Advanced Media

Mandatory units

1. Investigating the content of media products
2. Originating and producing print and graphics material
3. Planning and producing print and graphics products
4. Planning audio-visual production
5. Producing audio-visual products
6. Investigating and carrying out media research
7. Investigating and carrying out media marketing
8. Investigating media industries in the UK and abroad

Optional units

9. Researching for the media
10. Journalism
11. The medium of sound
12. Visual literacy

13. Narrative structure
14. Live television and radio
15. The individual as a media producer
16. Investigating advertising and communications

Core skills units

1. Application of Number
2. Communication
3. Information Technology

Science

Science GNVQs develop skills and understanding which are valuable in any field of scientific work. At Intermediate level you will learn how to plan and manage scientific tasks in a methodical way. You will use scientific methods to produce useful products – natural and artificial. And you will investigate the workings of systems – from the human body to a car engine.

At Advanced level you will develop understanding in scientific analysis and investigation of materials and systems. You will learn how energy can be converted and used, and how reactions are controlled. The programme emphasises the application of scientific skills and understanding in the world of real work.

Foundation Science

Mandatory units

1. Working on scientific tasks
2. Health and safety in science activities
3. Investigating working in science

Optional units

You will need to complete three optional units out of the six, which are common to all the awarding bodies.

4.* Contributing to a team activity
5. Growing, harvesting and processing
6. Repairing and maintaining things
7. Sport, leisure and health
8. Food science
9. Living things and materials in the environment

Core skills units

1. Application of Number
2. Communication
3. Information Technology

Intermediate Science

Mandatory units

1. Working on scientific tasks
2. Investigate living things, materials and substances
3. Make useful products
4. Monitor and control systems

Optional units

You will need to complete two optional units from a range of four. Each awarding body offers its own optional units.

Core skills units

1. Application of Number
2. Communication
3. Information Technology

Advanced Science

Mandatory units

1. Laboratory safety and analysis of samples
2. Investigate materials and their use

3. Obtain new substances
4. Obtain products from organisms
5. Control the transfer of energy
6. Control reactions
7. Human physiology and health care management
8. Communicating information

Optional units

You will need to complete four optional units from a range of about eight. Each awarding body offers its own optional units.

Core skills units

1. Application of Number
2. Communication
3. Information Technology

Core Skills – Skills for Life

6 What the economy needs are people who are numerate, literate and have what the CBI describes as "core skills" ... that is the ability to communicate, to apply technology, work with others, solve problems and to be able to respond to change.... I think industry can reasonably expect people to leave education at all levels with these skills.

Secretary of State for Education, 1992

This chapter explains the part that core skills play in GNVQ programmes.

It tells you:

- what core skills are
- why they are important
- what level of skill you must achieve
- how you should apply core skills
- how they are assessed
- how you can progress to core skills above the target level.

There are some skills that will serve you well whatever career you plan to take up. In almost any job you will be expected to:

- communicate clearly in speech and writing with colleagues and clients
- have basic competence in arithmetical calculations
- know how to handle and process information, using computers where necessary.

In addition, it would obviously be of advantage to yourself and your employer if you could:

➡ recognise practical problems and work out ways of solving them, either by yourself or with the aid of others

➡ demonstrate the kind of personal awareness that enables you to work well with people of different status and background

➡ recognise your own limitations and devise ways of improving your performance.

These are the kinds of basic skills that are essential not only for virtually all occupations, but also for life in general. They are core skills – personal, life-long skills which will make you more adaptable, responsible and self-confident.

For an example of how important core skills are, imagine that you are going for your first job interview at, say, a large travel agency. You have all the necessary formal qualifications (you wouldn't have been given the interview otherwise), but the candidate waiting ahead of you has even better grades and, what's more, is fluent in a foreign language. Why, then, have you been selected for interview? Obviously, your letter of application impressed the personnel manager, and now the interviewers want to test that impression.

What they will be looking for are qualities which are difficult to set down on paper. The interviewers will be looking to see if you express yourself clearly, listen attentively and respond appropriately. They will encourage you to be positive about your talents, but they might also expect you to point out any relevant limitations (that missing foreign language) and indicate how you might make up for them. They will be interested to see if you are at ease with strangers (none of the interviewers will be known to you), and they will want to reassure themselves that you can work as part of a team.

In short, they will be testing your personal skills – in particular, your ability to communicate. Some people seem to be natural communicators, but most of us could benefit from a practical programme to help us express ourselves more clearly and confidently. The Communication core skill in GNVQ programmes has been designed to do just that.

GNVQs and core skills areas

Communication is just one of the core skills developed in all GNVQ programmes. Altogether, there are six core skills units, each offered at five different levels. Although these are numbered, not named, core skills at levels 1, 2 or 3 correspond respectively to Foundation, Intermediate and Advanced. The specifications of each core skill at any particular level are exactly the same across all the vocational areas.

1 **Communication:** the ability to write and talk appropriately for a particular purpose and audience, and to understand and interpret information through reading and listening.

2 **Application of Number:** the ability to use a range of fundamental arithmetical and statistical techniques to reach conclusions in practical situations.

3 **Information Technology:** the ability to use computers to sort, process and retrieve information and to present information in forms appropriate to purpose and audience.

4 **Personal Skills – Improving Own Learning and Performance:** the ability to learn and to improve performance.

5 **Personal Skills – Working with Others:** the ability to work independently and as part of a team, and to use self-awareness to guide action.

6 Problem-solving: the ability to identify and evaluate the nature of problems and devise approaches to address them; to plan, implement and evaluate the effectiveness of problem-solving approaches.

Communication, Application of Number and Information Technology are *mandatory core skills* units in all GNVQs, and it is these skills which this chapter focuses on.

Personal Skills and Problem-solving are not requirements for the award of a GNVQ – although the programmes will provide opportunities for students to achieve in these areas. The two Personal Skills units count as additional units; if you pass them, the achievement will be recorded on your GNVQ certificate. Problem-solving has not yet been accredited, but GNVQ centres are encouraged to assess achievement in this core skill and to record the achievement in the student's National Record of Achievement.

The minimum requirements

To gain a GNVQ at any level, you must achieve the three mandatory core skills units at the same or a higher level. If you are taking an Intermediate GNVQ, you must achieve Communication, Application of Number and Information Technology at level 2 or above. At Advanced level, you will need level 3 core skills units or better.

Mandatory core skills themes

Core skills units are set out in the same way as the vocational units. They are made up of *elements* (which describe the activity to be assessed), *performance criteria* (which describe what you must do in order to meet the requirements of the element), and *range statements* (which describe the required depth and extent of coverage).

Progression up the levels is marked by:

- a broadening of the range in which the core skill must be applied
- increasing complexity
- increasing student independence.

But at all levels, the elements in a particular core skills unit will cover the same themes. Here are the main themes of the three mandatory core skills units.

Communication

The units in Communication identify four key themes:

- taking part in discussions
- preparing written materials
- using images to illustrate points made in writing and discussions
- reading and responding to written materials and images.

As you progress up the levels, you will be required to demonstrate increasing sophistication of performance through more complex activities. At level 1, for example, your discussions will be with people who are familiar with the subject matter and with whom you are in frequent contact – fellow students or tutors, probably. At level 3, you will also be required to take part in discussions with strangers – customers, clients or visitors – who are not familiar with the subject matter.

Application of Number

The units in Application of Number identify three key themes:

- gathering and processing data
- representing and tackling problems
- interpreting and presenting data.

As you progress up the levels, you will find that the mathematical techniques involved become more complex. For example, at level 1, 'Represent and tackle problems' will involve using:

- addition, subtraction, multiplication and division
- fractions, decimals and percentages
- simple formulae
- finding perimeters, areas and volumes
- using 2-D co-ordinates.

At level 3, you will supplement these techniques with others, including:

- calculating with fractions, percentages and ratios
- carrying out calculations relating to plane and solid shapes
- using co-ordinates to locate position in 3-D.

Information Technology
The units in Information Technology identify five key themes:

- storing and inputting information
- editing and organising information
- presenting information
- evaluating procedures and features of application
- dealing with errors and faults.

As you progress up the levels, you will be required to apply a greater range of information technology, and to perform increasingly complex operations.

Links with the National Curriculum

The GNVQ core skills levels broadly correspond with the ten-level framework of the National Curriculum (see overleaf).

GNVQ level	Core skills level	National Curriculum level
Foundation	1	4 and below
Intermediate	2	5 and 6
Advanced	3	7
	4	8 and 9
	5	10 and above

The linkage between mathematics in the National Curriculum and the Application of Number core skills unit is very precise, and there is also a close relationship between English and Communication. So why, you may ask, are GCSEs in mathematics and English not automatically accepted as evidence of attainment in Application of Number and Communication? The answer is that GNVQ core skills must be demonstrated in *practical situations*. For example, a requirement of level 3 Communication is that you participate in discussions with a range of audiences – not an activity that is emphasised in GCSE English. However, there may be appropriate evidence from GCSEs or other sources which can be presented for recognition against core skills units. Appropriate evidence, in this case, means that it matches the detail of the unit specifications.

Integrated skills

Here is an example of a core skills element, taken from the level 2 unit in Communication:

Element 2.1: Take part in discussions with a range of people on routine matters

Performance criteria

1 Own contributions are clear and appropriate to the subject matter.

2 Own contributions are made in a tone and manner suited to the audience.

3 Contributions from others are listened to attentively.

4 Own understanding of points made by others is actively checked and confirmed.

Range

Subject matters: routine matters (eg responding to day-to-day enquiries; discussing routine tasks)

Mode: face to face; using the telephone

Audience: people familiar with the subject matter and in frequent contact with the individual (eg supervisors, colleagues, peers, tutors); people familiar with the subject matter but not in frequent contact with the individual (eg some customers/clients)

The specification of this unit is the same for all Intermediate vocational programmes, which is why the subject of the discussion is not specified. That does not mean the discussion can be about anything; it should be relevant to the vocational area.

Core skills should be integrated as far as possible within the programme you are following – that is, they should be applied and assessed within the context of your projects and activities. An NCVQ guide to assessing core skills explains the importance of Communication and the importance of assessing the skills within the context of an activity.

We use communication skills all the time, often without thinking consciously about the strategies we are using and how they might be improved. The core skills units provide a description of what makes up effective communication. They can help students to stop and think about the skills and strategies they use, and compare what they do now with what they might do in new, unfamiliar settings. It is obviously not enough to just *think* about what you might do in new, unfamiliar settings, it is important to have a go at communicating in them.

Assessing Core Skills in GNVQs, NCVQ, 1993

Whatever occupational programme you are following, your projects and assignments should give you many opportunities to acquire and demonstrate core skills. For example, the following element in Intermediate Manufacturing involves a number of core skills:

Element 2.3: Prepare production schedules

Performance criteria

1 Type and quantity of production resource requirements are accurately detailed.
2 For each production stage, costs are accurately calculated.
3 Time required for each production stage is accurately calculated.
4 Schedule is presented in a style appropriate to the sector.

Range

Resources: capital (eg plant, machinery, equipment); human (eg health and safety); material (eg availability)
Presentation: manual, computer-based
Key production stages: material preparation; processing; assembly; finishing; packaging

From this specification, you can see that Application of Number is required to analyse information and perform calculations on time and cost; and that Communication is necessary to gather verbal or written information and to present findings. If the findings are presented to an unfamiliar audience – perhaps the production manager of a local manufacturing company – then they will have covered some of the more demanding parts of the range in the Communication units. In addition, there is scope to use information technology to analyse data, produce statistics and write up findings.

The vocational units do not state which core skills elements, if any, can be matched to the performance criteria or range statements. That does not mean you will be left frantically guessing where the core skills evidence might be lurking. At most GNVQ centres, the tutors will have drawn up plans which identify where opportunities for assessing core skills can be scheduled into the programme. When you are given projects or assignments, your tutors will point out the core skills elements which you can pick up during your tasks. In most centres, your assignment sheets (page 32) will list which core skills elements can be matched to particular tasks. With experience, you should start recognising opportunities to use core skills that might otherwise have been missed.

Most elements of the vocational units will present opportunities for you to collect evidence of core skills, but don't expect to meet all the requirements for a core skills unit from a single assignment. As with the vocational units, core skills attainment is progressive, with evidence being accumulated from a variety of different projects. That makes it essential for you to keep track of your progress. Your tutor will help you plan a campaign of action so that you will be better able to achieve the necessary units by the end of your programme.

Problems and solutions

Students who have not been successful in GCSE mathematics may be daunted by the Application of Number core skill. In fact, many students have been pleasantly surprised to find that mathematics suddenly begins to make sense when it is applied to practical problems.

Most schools and colleges will provide workshops and extra lessons for students who are weak in basic numeracy and information technology skills. Some centres provide regular sessions several times a week, with students dropping in as necessary. Of course, the skills which are learnt through these sessions should then be applied and assessed in the context of the GNVQ programme.

Some students have found it difficult to apply some of the core skills in a practical context. Although all the vocational areas offer the opportunity to demonstrate core skills across the range, some areas are likely to promote more advanced achievements in one or more core skills – for example, Communication in Health and Social Care, Application of Number in Science. In the trial year of GNVQs, this led some centres to push the definition of 'vocational context' to its limits – and perhaps beyond. At one school, business students demonstrated their knowledge of Pythagoras's theorem by measuring the angles of a window-cleaner's ladder; the Health and Social Care students applied the same calculations to a triangular bandage.

Activity

A GNVQ tutor acknowledged the problem and explained how his college dealt with it.

> We try to deliver most of the core skills through the assignments, but some of them – particularly numeracy – we find we just can't put into a vocational context. It's silly tying yourself into knots making a student demonstrate a skill in a totally meaningless context. Instead, we're setting up core skills workshops across the college. All GNVQ students attend these, which are led by specialists in the different core skills. They have developed packages or pieces of work integrating core skills, so when a student comes along and says they are having trouble getting this particular piece of this core skill, the tutor will give them the package, tell them to work through it and then present the work for assessment.

Many centres now call on specialist help, particularly from maths and information technology teachers, to build opportunities and activities within the vocational areas where particular core skills have genuine relevance.

One way of mopping up Application of Number skills that might otherwise be missed is to include survey work in GNVQ areas.

Finally, if you are nearing the end of your programme and are still missing some core skills elements, don't panic. If they cannot reasonably be put into a vocational context, it is acceptable to cover them on their own.

Assessment

You will be relieved to know that there are no external tests of core skills. Basically, core skills are assessed in the same way as the vocational units, with the internal assessors using the same methods:

- scrutiny of written materials, such as log books, reports, questionnaires
- scrutiny of artefacts, eg a model
- observation of student performing an activity, such as an interview or a commentary
- oral questioning
- written questioning.

All of this evidence may come from the activities under-taken on your GNVQ programme, but there is no reason why valid evidence shouldn't be accepted from any part of your learning – work experience, personal interests or prior learning.

In some cases, you might be confident that you have a good grasp of a skill, but if the assessor is not sure, you might be asked to apply the same skill in another setting. Alternatively, you might be asked questions designed to establish whether you could demonstrate the skill consist-ently in a variety of contexts.

Like individual vocational units, the core skills units are not graded. If you meet the target level, your achievement will be credited and will count towards the full GNVQ award. If you do not meet the level, you may still have gained enough evidence to be awarded units at a lower level.

Progressing to higher levels

There are no rules that prevent you from achieving a core skills unit above the target level set for your GNVQ. Since each level includes every aspect of the unit at all the levels below it, progression up the levels basically involves build-ing on the same skills and applying them in a wider range of contexts. It is worth looking at the greater demands for the higher level to see if they are within your scope, but even if you feel capable of tackling them, there may be practical reasons why it is not possible to achieve a higher core skills level within a single GNVQ programme.

'The problem is', a tutor explains, 'that a student who has sailed through Communication in a term may be in a group with members who are struggling with that core skill. Since the whole group is following the same programme, it can be difficult organising assignments to suit both the highly proficient and the less proficient students.

'Even so, we encourage students to achieve core skills at higher levels, if possible.'

4 Some Questions Answered

Interviewer: 'Do your tutors explain the terms used in GNVQs?'
Student: 'Yes – when they understand them themselves.'

This chapter gives you the answers to a wide range of questions.

You will find out:

- ↦ what to do if you have to move house in the middle of your programme
- ↦ whether you can take a foreign language as part of your GNVQ
- ↦ whether you can take GNVQs before the age of 16
- ↦ what students like about GNVQs – and what they don't like.

IMPORTANT!

- ↦ Policies and practices vary widely among the different GNVQ centres, so treat the answers as a starting point only – as a list to remind you of the sort of things you should be asking yourself and your teachers before you make any final decisions about enrolling for a GNVQ programme.
- ↦ There are also a few statistics, but they don't tell the whole story. They were collected during the introductory phase, when the number of centres and subjects was limited and the programmes themselves were still being developed.

No doubt, questions such as 'what qualifications will I need?', and 'where should I take a GNVQ?' have already occurred to you. Answers to these and a whole range of other common queries are given below, together with answers to some questions you probably haven't thought of. Much of the information given here is covered more fully elsewhere in this book.

Q What qualifications will I need?

A 'We outlined (to the students) the two levels available and offered the general guidelines that students studying Intermediate level would have Ds and Es at GCSE, while students studying Advanced level would have at least four or five GCSE higher grades (A–C). We stressed the type of work involved and related this to GCSE coursework.'

GNVQ tutor

There are no firm and fixed requirements for entry to GNVQ programmes, but obviously your tutors will want to be satisfied that you have the ability to successfully complete a particular programme. In the introductory year, most schools adopted a flexible attitude, demanding lower entry requirements than for AS and GCE A-level courses. As the qualification becomes established, entry requirements will probably become more demanding, with only Foundation students being offered open access to the programme.

At Intermediate level, entry qualifications in the introductory year ranged from none to a minimum of four Es at GCSE.

A few students with poor previous achievements were admitted to Advanced programmes on the strength of diagnostic tests and evaluation, but most centres set minimum requirements, ranging from two Cs at GCSE (usually in maths and English) to four Cs and better. These entry qualifications were exceeded by many students, including a fair number with eight or nine A–Cs at GCSE. Some schools said that all their Advanced GNVQ students were capable of taking GCE A-levels.

The table below shows the qualifications held by GNVQ students at 24 schools and colleges in the introductory year. No distinction is made between students studying at different levels, or students with more than one type of qualification.

Qualifications	Number of students
5 or more GCSEs grades A–C	376
Fewer than 5 GCSEs grades A–C	1,356
BTEC First	263
City and Guilds Foundation	56
CPVE	11
A-level	3
NVQ level 3	34
No formal qualifications	4

Finally, this is what one GNVQ tutor had to say about entry requirements:

‘ We set no entry requirements for Foundation level, but we make it clear what the programme entails, stressing the fact that it isn't an easy option and that it's a knowledge-based programme, not a practical skills course.

'For the Intermediate programme, quite a few students will exceed our minimum entry requirement of two Cs at GCSE, but we have to evaluate the suitability of each student individually, because some of them who meet the entry requirement may struggle with the core skills.

'We set a requirement of four or five Cs at GCSE for entry to Advanced – the same as for A-level students. Having said that, we would look favourably at applications from some of our students who might get only two or three Cs but who are very interested in the GNVQ programme. In the end, it's the student's motivation that counts. Those who want to do well and who are interested in their course will succeed. The same goes for A-level students, and also for university students.

Q Do I have to take Foundation first and work my way up to Advanced?

A No. Assuming that you have the appropriate entry qualifications, the choice of level is up to you. If you plan to progress into higher education, you should certainly consider taking Advanced. At some colleges, GNVQ entrants are not allocated to a particular level until they have completed a three- to six-week induction programme, which allows their tutors to assess their abilities.

Do not assume that, because you have the entry requirements for a particular level, you will find the work easy. In the introductory year, quite a few Intermediate students said that they found the programme too demanding and would have preferred to have done a Foundation programme first.

Q How many GNVQs should I take?

A Intermediate is designed to be broadly equivalent to four GCSEs, while Advanced is the equivalent of two GCE A-levels. On that basis alone, each programme should take up about half your timetable, so obviously there would be practical constraints on doing more than two GNVQs simultaneously.

Most students take only one GNVQ at a time, with or without another qualification. In a sample of 1,532 GNVQ students, all but 22 were taking one GNVQ at either Intermediate or Advanced. Only seven students were taking two Intermediate GNVQs, four were taking two Advanced GNVQs, while 11 were combining two different GNVQs at Intermediate and Advanced.

Q Can I combine a GNVQ with other qualifications?

A Yes, and most students do. The following statement is typical of the policy adopted by many schools: 'All students are able to "mix and match" GCE A-level/AS, GCSE and GNVQ. This flexibility causes problems with timetabling but gives the students the opportunity to study GNVQs with complementary subjects. It also enables students to remain as integrated members of the sixth form rather than as a discrete group.'

GCSEs are the most popular additional studies at Intermediate, while many Advanced students aiming to go on to higher education take one GNVQ in conjunction with one GCE A-level. A small number of exceptional students are taking two GCE A-levels in conjunction with an Advanced GNVQ.

Some college centres that specialise in vocational qualifications do not offer a wide range of GCE A-level courses to GNVQ students. Instead, Advanced GNVQ students can enhance the value of their qualification by taking additional GNVQ units within the same vocational area, or from another area. Six additional units are considered broadly equivalent to one GCE A-level. Most of the additional units have been adapted from other tried and tested vocational courses, and though none of them has as yet been accredited by the NCVQ, many higher education institutions recognise them as entrance qualifications. Chapter 8 tells you all about GNVQs and progression to higher education.

> # IMPORTANT!
>
> ↦ GNVQs are flexible enough to fit in neatly with other courses, but the demands of a GCE A-level timetable may restrict the opportunities for work placement on a GNVQ programme.

When choosing additional studies, take into account your own abilities, interests and aspirations. Provided that your interests are matched by your abilities, it is probably better to complement and extend your knowledge than to cover similar ground with a different qualification.

For example, a Business GNVQ with a GCE A-level in accounting or computing might be a stronger combination than a Business GNVQ and GCE A-level business studies. The choice is yours, but don't overload yourself simply because you think that a particular combination of qualifications would look good to a prospective employer or admissions tutor. It's better to be realistic about your capabilities, like the GNVQ Business student who admitted: 'I'm not really cut out for higher education. I feel I'd be better sticking to the original 12 units than stretching myself so far that I end up with nothing.'

Q Can I take a foreign language as part of my GNVQ programme?

A Language units are available as optional units in some programmes, including Business, Hospitality and

Catering, and Leisure and Tourism. But they can be taken as additional units in other areas. Some centres offer different language courses rather than GNVQ units. A language qualification would be a useful addition to any GNVQ.

Q Can I take only part of a GNVQ?

A It is likely that students choosing GNVQ pre-16 would take only part of the programme – either a group of specified units, or one or two units of their own choosing.

Usually, older full-time students would only take part of a GNVQ in conjunction with other studies, but some colleges are establishing part-time programmes which they expect will have particular appeal to mature students. Provided you complete at least one unit, you will be credited for each unit you have achieved. This applies not only to students who choose to do only one or two units, but also to students who fail to achieve the full award.

Q I want to take a Manufacturing GNVQ and GCE A-levels. My local college offers this GNVQ, but my school doesn't. The trouble is, I'd prefer to stay at my school if possible because I think it offers the best chance of my getting good GCE A-levels. Does this mean I should forget the idea of a Manufacturing GNVQ?

A This is a tricky one. Most GNVQ centres don't have the resources to offer all the available GNVQs, which limits choices, especially if there are other important factors to consider, as in your case. However, in some areas, schools and colleges are collaborating so that students at one institution can take courses or parts of courses at another school or college.

Q Where should I take GNVQ – at school or college?

A The awarding bodies make sure that all GNVQ centres deliver the programmes to the necessary standards. So, strictly from that point of view, it doesn't matter whether you take your GNVQ programme at school, sixth-form college or a further education centre. There are, however, many factors which could influence your choice – some purely personal or social, some practical and some a combination of the two.

Assuming that you have a choice between two or more centres, all of which offer the basic GNVQ programme that interests you, consider what else each has to offer in the way of 'extras'. After doing this, it may be that the over-riding factor that determines your choice has got nothing to do with GNVQs; it may be that you choose a centre on the strength of its sporting facilities or the fact that your best friend is a student there. That's fine; at least you will have considered all the options. What you don't want to do is to sign up for the first available programme without thought, and then, weeks or months later, find out that another GNVQ centre is offering a menu more suited to your tastes. The attractions of staying on in school are obvious. You will be:

- in a familiar environment
- among old friends
- taught by teachers who know you and who are aware of your individual abilities.

Being in the sixth form may confer status and privileges:

- no uniform
- your own common room
- fewer restrictions on personal transport.

GNVQ sixthformers in particular will probably broaden their horizons through links with higher education institutions, and through the contacts with local businesses and industry that are organised as part of most GNVQ programmes.

IMPORTANT!

➡ Consider the travelling arrangements you may have to make to get to college. A 20-mile journey by public transport may not be too bad in summer, but you might find it unbearable in the dark and cold of winter. One rural school a long way from the nearest further education college welcomed GNVQs because of the high drop-out rate of former students who simply couldn't face the daily journey to and from college.

From the personal and social point of view, going to a further education college has its appeal, too. Although quite a few of your friends will probably be going with you, the change from school to college is:

➡ a step towards independence and adulthood
➡ an opportunity to meet and make friends with people from outside your own circle – people from a variety of backgrounds, of different ages and experience, who will stimulate and broaden your own interests.

College versus school

Let's assume that, long journey or short, your main concern is to get on a GNVQ programme that's right for you. Your school offers the GNVQ you're interested in and so does your local further education college.

Many colleges and fewer schools have long experience of teaching a range of vocational courses at a range of levels. Many of their teaching staff have direct experience of the relevant vocational areas. For example, at one college the Leisure and Tourism team included tutors who had worked in the hotel and catering industries. Apart from being able to teach from experience, such tutors can be invaluable in organising projects and assignments with genuine occupational relevance.

Another claim often made by large colleges offering a very wide range of qualifications is that each of their GNVQ programmes is delivered by a team of specialists – four, five or even more tutors, each responsible for a different aspect of the programme, not just one or two individual teachers covering the entire area. This sounds most attractive, but at one college the Advanced Business students complained that they had too many tutors, none of whom seemed to be communicating with the others. The progressive structure of a GNVQ programme makes it important for the work to be clearly co-ordinated, so it is not necessarily a bad thing to be in daily contact with only a couple of teachers.

It's impossible to generalise about the facilities that different centres are able to offer, but one college geared to vocational courses did point out that it was able to provide some GNVQ students with work experience 'in-house' – in canteens, bars, etc.

REMEMBER !

➤➤ As you can imagine, the list of variables is long. The best way of finding out which centre is right for you is to talk to your own teachers and also visit a college on one of its open days. Try to get all the information you need well before you have to make a choice. One or two students spoke of being pressurised by being told that if they did not enrol for a course quickly, they wouldn't get a place on it.

Another consideration is what other courses of study are offered. If you plan to take GCE A-levels with GNVQs, you might be better off staying at a school with long experience of teaching this course. On the other hand, some colleges offer a very wide range of additional GNVQ units or other vocational courses, including NVQs.

Q My friends doing GCE A-levels say GNVQ is a 'Mickey Mouse' course. Is it?

A Presumably, they mean it's some kind of soft option. If they were to take a serious look at GNVQs, they would change their uninformed minds. Read the following comments from a group of school students, one of whom has nine A–Cs at GCSE and is combining Advanced GNVQ with two GCE A-levels:

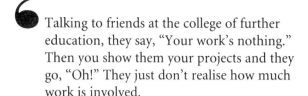

Talking to friends at the college of further education, they say, "Your work's nothing." Then you show them your projects and they go, "Oh!" They just don't realise how much work is involved.

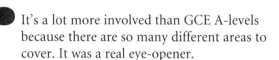

It's a lot more involved than GCE A-levels because there are so many different areas to cover. It was a real eye-opener.

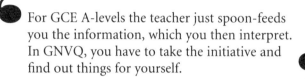

For GCE A-levels the teacher just spoon-feeds you the information, which you then interpret. In GNVQ, you have to take the initiative and find out things for yourself.

Q Does that mean that GNVQs are difficult?

A Every worthwhile course should stretch you, and GNVQ is no exception. But one of the good features of the GNVQ programme is that it allows you to work towards the full award at your own pace. That said, you will be set deadlines for some of your projects and assignments, and you should be aware of the demands that a GNVQ programme will make on your time.

You don't really appreciate how big the course is until you're halfway through, but you ought to know how much work is involved from day one and knuckle down from the start. It's no good thinking, "Oh, I'll get that unit covered soon enough."

An Intermediate Business student

A GNVQ teacher makes another point: 'We made it clear that it was likely that pupils who disliked GCSE coursework and taking personal responsibility for its completion and who failed to meet the coursework deadlines would not make good GNVQ students.'

Q If that's the case, why have I been offered the chance to do a GNVQ, but not a GCE A-level?

A The two qualifications emphasise different aptitudes. As a crude distinction, GCE A-levels require a high level of reading and writing skills, plus the ability to think analytically, while GNVQs are more concerned with the application of general skills and knowledge in a vocational context. Some students possess both types of skill; others are stronger in one or the other.

I'd recommend GNVQs to anyone struggling with GCE A-levels. Frankly, the reason I came on this course was I don't think I'm good enough for GCE A-levels. This is a different method of learning – much more vocational, which suits me well. I'm definitely better at coursework than exams.

A GNVQ Business student

Q But aren't there exams for GNVQs?

A There are no end-of-course examinations, as in GCE A-levels. There are one-hour tests for each GNVQ mandatory unit. These consist of multiple-choice questions and are set at frequent intervals throughout the programme, with several opportunities to sit each test, if necessary. A pass in each test is an essential requirement for the full award.

Q Why is the pass mark for GNVQ tests nearly twice as high as it is for GCE A-levels?

A In GNVQs, you will be tested on knowledge which is considered essential across a broad vocational area. The questions are multiple-choice, so you will not be asked to justify your answers or marshal complicated arguments. GCE A-level examinations test knowledge much more closely, in more detail, and demand greater evidence of analytical thinking.

Q Is there a high drop-out rate?

A During the first two years of GNVQ, a disappointingly high number of students failed to finish their programmes or simply dropped out.

There were several reasons for the high drop-out rate:

●▸ Some students found their programme unsuitable and/or too demanding. If you do find a particular level too difficult, you should be able to transfer to a lower level, taking with you evidence towards the other qualification.

●▸ Quite a few students had been transferred to GNVQ from other vocational courses halfway through the academic year and were therefore not voluntary recruits. Some of them thought that the new programmes would qualify them for specific jobs – eg sports teacher or physiotherapist – and were disappointed to find that GNVQs are not occupation-specific qualifications. With the introduction of GNVQs for 14- to 16-year olds, new students will have a much clearer idea of what their programmes involve, and where they can lead.

●▸ Some students – and teachers – had unrealistic ideas about the amount of work involved in a GNVQ programme. Students were allowed to work at their own pace and, in some cases, simply ran out of time. There is now a better understanding of the demands of GNVQ programmes, and though to some extent you can set your on pace, you will be expected to meet deadlines for GNVQ work.

Students have dropped out at Foundation level for a number of reasons. You can learn from their mistakes:

➡ Don't assume Foundation level is practical – it's not. There is a lot of knowledge to gain.
➡ Work training may be a better option for you – consider it if you want to do something practical.
➡ You will have to get to grips with the terms used to describe the work and assessments.

Q Which is the most popular GNVQ subject?

A Meaningful comparisons cannot be made until all 15 planned GNVQs have become established. Even then, the numbers doing a particular GNVQ will not be a guide to its worth. In rural areas, the GNVQ in Land-based Industries should attract many students, but it is highly unlikely that this GNVQ will be offered in the majority of GNVQ centres.

Just to satisfy your curiosity, here is the breakdown of subject choice among the 81,673 students registered for Intermediate and Advanced GNVQs during the autumn of 1993:

Business	34,423
Health and Social Care	18,425
Leisure and Tourism	14,462
Art and Design	9,073
Manufacturing	1,790

In addition, about 5,000 students were involved in the piloting of Foundation GNVQs in these areas, and another 3,500 were involved in the piloting of GNVQs in Intermediate and Advanced Construction and the Built Environment, Hospitality and Catering, and Science.

Q Why are so few students taking Manufacturing?

A Perhaps the small intake reflects the declining importance of manufacturing in the national economy. Students may not feel that a career in manufacturing offers the same prospects or security that they would hope to find in another sector. This is a great pity.

According to one senior educationalist, 'The Manufacturing GNVQ is a very good GNVQ for aspiring engineers because it develops attributes and skills which GCE A-levels would find difficult to develop. They're relevant.'

A college tutor echoed this view, but also expressed the opinion that the qualification was too general. 'It's a good course,' he said, 'but it doesn't hit the mark. The main problem is that it's not industry-specific, and as yet we don't know how interchangeable it would be across the whole range of the manufacturing industry. Here, we're planning a Manufacturing programme that focuses on print and media. At the end of it, the students should have a qualification relevant to the printing and media industries, but I don't know how acceptable it would be to a manufacturing firm in another industry.'

Q I've set my heart on going to university. I'd like to take a GNVQ, but I'm worried that it won't be considered seriously as an entrance qualification. Should I forget a GNVQ and concentrate on GCE A-levels?

A The subject of GNVQs and access to higher
education, including degree courses, is covered in
chapter 8. Perhaps the simplest way to answer your
question, though, is to point out that more than 80
per cent of GNVQ students from the first Advanced
programmes were offered conditional places at higher
education institutions, including universities. A Pass
at Advanced can secure a place on degree courses, but
your choice of institutions and/or courses will be
increased if you have a Merit or Distinction, plus
additional qualifications. Additional GNVQ units
meet the requirements of many universities, but
admissions tutors at some institutions that attract
many candidates ask for a GCE A-level, sometimes in
a specified subject and at a particular grade.

Because GCE A-levels are understood and
accepted by all universities, they are still probably a
safer bet than GNVQs. Safer, but by no means sure.
Competition for university places is intense, and even
good grades in three GCE A-levels are not a cast-iron
guarantee of admission to the degree course and/or
university of your choice.

Q How highly are GNVQs valued by employers?

A This is a variant of the previous question, and the
answer follows the same lines. GNVQs are being
enthusiastically backed and promoted by the CBI, the
trades unions and the Department of Employment.
When their value becomes more widely known
among employers, possessing a GNVQ in the relevant
area should give you an edge over other job
applicants. For some jobs, a relevant GNVQ may be
more highly valued than a GCE A-level. Your GNVQ
programme should certainly increase your knowledge,
understanding and skills required in certain
occupations.

Q It's the vocational aspect that interests me. Will I be given actual work experience?

A The provision of work experience varies between centres. An early survey showed that more than three-quarters of the students in Business, Health and Social Care, and Leisure and Tourism received work-based experience, while rather less than half the students in Art and Design and Manufacturing were given work placements.

Whether or not you receive work experience, you will almost certainly visit businesses and industries in the course of your assignments, and you will probably receive talks or lectures from experts in your vocational area. At many centres, especially further education colleges, your tutors will have worked in the areas they now teach.

Remember that GNVQs are designed to develop skills and knowledge within a broad vocational area, not to develop competence in a particular job. If you want most of your learning to come from the workplace, you should consider taking an alternative or additional qualification, such as an NVQ. Some centres are considering developing the option of a combined GNVQ/NVQ programme that involves a weekly schedule of three days at school and two days in the workplace. Another option, available from September 1995, is the Modern Apprenticeship scheme which trains entrants to NVQ level 3 or above. The scheme is aimed at 16- to 17-year-olds – either school-leavers with no vocational qualifications or students who might have taken Foundation or Intermediate GNVQ. Modern Apprenticeships and NVQs are explained in chapter 5.

Q Will I have to pay for my GNVQ course?

A Most education authorities fund further education programmes for students between the ages of 16 and

19, but policies do vary. Some authorities provide students with credits for two years' further education, which should cover the whole Advanced GNVQ programme. But if you want to transfer to an Advanced GNVQ after completing a year on another course, you might not receive a grant to cover the full programme. Check the funding implications with your teachers or local authority.

Q Are there any textbooks for my GNVQ programme?

A Most current GNVQ publications are designed to help teachers deliver the programmes, but several students' handbooks to some of the vocational areas have been published, and more are in the pipeline.

Remember that though the requirements for each GNVQ are very precise, it's up to you and your tutors to decide how they should be tackled. With guidance from your tutors, you will be expected to take responsibility for your own learning, which means that you will have to investigate where knowledge and information can be found, rather than relying on textbooks. As one student said: 'You have to find out things for yourself, which makes it a bit harder but more interesting.'

Q I don't have computer skills. Are they necessary?

A Computer skills are called for in the Information Technology core skills unit, and they are extremely useful for recording, processing and presenting the information you will collect on your assignments. GNVQ students who lack computer skills will usually be taught them at the beginning of the programme.

Q I've looked at the unit specifications for my GNVQ and I couldn't understand them. How will I cope?

A There are a lot of new ideas and terms to grasp, but they will be explained to you before you start your programme. Most schools run bridging courses for students going on to GNVQs, while colleges organise induction programmes for GNVQ entrants. In the meantime, you'll find all the unfamiliar terms explained in this book – where they first occur, and in the glossary at the end.

Q Can I take a GNVQ in Year 11?

A Changes in the National Curriculum requirement mean that schools can offer GNVQs and possibly NVQs to 14- to 16-year-olds. NCVQ strongly advises that only schools with the necessary resources and staff trained to deliver vocational education should offer GNVQs, so it may be a year or two before the qualification is generally available in Year 11.

Because Foundation and Intermediate GNVQs both cover the ground of about four GCSEs, it would be difficult to take either of the complete programmes without crowding out other studies. It is possible that some schools would offer a full programme by using time outside the National Curriculum, but in practice, most pre-16 students would take some Foundation or Intermediate GNVQ units as qualifications in their own right. If they wished, they could then continue towards the full award post 16.

There is some overlap between GNVQ core skills and GCSEs, particularly in maths. This raises the possibility of students gaining awards in GCSEs and GNVQ units for the same course.

Q Will my parents understand GNVQs?

A If they make the effort. This is what one student had to say:

I tried to explain the course to my dad, but he didn't have a clue what I was on about. My mother found it a bit difficult too, but when she finally cracked it, she thought it was a good idea. She said she wished they'd had GNVQs when she was at school.

Q You say that I can do a GNVQ at my own pace. Does that mean it doesn't matter if I don't finish my programme in the time allowed?

A That depends on your aims. Although GNVQs have a flexible timetable compared with other courses, students aiming to progress to other full-time courses should make every effort to finish Foundation and Intermediate programmes within one year, and to complete an Advanced programme within two years. When GNVQs were new and untried, quite a few students failed to complete their programmes in the allotted time and were allowed to complete their work in the summer holidays or return to school the following year. As the qualification becomes established, however, GNVQ centres will find it more difficult to accommodate students who fall seriously behind in their programmes.

However, it's important to remember that GNVQ is a progressive qualification, and that individual units are credited as well as the full award. Some students won't expect to achieve the full award within the recommended time. Guided by their teachers, they will try to achieve a reasonable number of unit credits, plus core skills. If they are going into a job, possibly with part-time further education, they might complete their GNVQ after leaving school.

Q I've been working for a year in a sports centre. Can I use my experience there as evidence?

A Yes, provided that it's relevant, and that it can be authenticated. General experience in an occupation may not be enough to meet the very precise specifications of a GNVQ.

Q I want to drop one of my two GCE A-levels and transfer to Advanced GNVQ. Can I do the programme in one year?

A You would find the workload heavy, especially with that GCE A-level, but it has been done successfully. Discuss the issue with your teachers.

Q I think that I've already covered some of my GNVQ requirements in GCSEs. Will this count towards the award?

A The NCVQ has said that evidence from GCSEs or other courses can count towards core skills units. However, the evidence must match the requirements set out in the units.

Q Can I take a GNVQ part-time?

A Yes, though only a few centres are offering this option at present.

Q My family is thinking of moving house halfway through the academic year. What happens if I have to leave my GNVQ programme before I have completed it?

A Because GNVQ work involves carefully planned and closely assessed assignments, it would be difficult (though not impossible) to complete a programme on your own. If there is no GNVQ centre near your new home, you face problems.

If there's another GNVQ centre, you can join and you can take unit credits with you. You can also transfer the evidence you have already gained from one programme to another. But if you are only part way through several units, it might be difficult to pick up where you left off. You might find that you have to go over ground you have already covered.

Explain the problem to your parents and, if you do have to move, talk it over with your teachers. At the very least, they should be able to restructure your programme so that by the time you leave you will have completed work on whole units.

Q What happens if I finish my GNVQ early?

A You could increase the value of your qualification by taking some additional units, or by progressing to core skills units at a higher level.

Students' views of GNVQs

The following quotes give an idea of what students themselves feel about aspects of GNVQs.

Some things students don't like about GNVQs or would prefer to see changed

Unit end tests

 I was told they weren't important, but then I realised that if you don't pass them, you won't pass the course. Every four months or so they keep springing these tests on you.

Unsuitable teachers

 Most of our tutors are fine, but there's one lecturer who hasn't adapted to GNVQs. He's more of an A-level teacher, expecting you to learn masses of stuff from books instead of letting you find out for yourself through projects.

Jargon/'unfriendly English'

 The language is a turn-off. You wouldn't know from the specs [unit specifications] that it's actually an interesting course.

Doubts about access to higher education

 They [the universities] might give you an interview, but whether they give you a place is another thing. My feeling is that if there are two candidates, one with three A-levels and the other with one A-level and an Advanced GNVQ, they'd give the place to the one with the three A-levels.

Paperwork

There's too much paperwork, too much cross-referencing, especially if a project covers more than one unit. There are too many forms to fill in.

Insufficient work experience

Work experience should be an essential part of a GNVQ programme.

Grading system

I don't really think much of the grades. I mean, if you go to an employer and say, "I've got a Distinction," he'll say, "What's that?" It's not like an A at A-level. I'd like to see the same grading system as is used for A-levels.

Some things students like about GNVQs

Everything

It's really good. It's so different from GCSEs. There's nothing I don't like.

Sense of personal achievement

You know that you get credit for the work that you've done yourself, not for something you've learnt from your teacher.

Independence

 I thought I was going to be stuck in a classroom being lectured at. Instead, I do most of the work outside the classroom.

 I like working independently, and at my own pace.

 I like being able to work on my own.

 It's good to get out and about, and to plan your own work.

A teacher emphasised that:

 one of the rewarding aspects of the course is how it helps students develop as individuals, with the ability to work things out for themselves.

Respect

 I find that teachers give more respect to GNVQ students. When they talk about A-level students, they still call them "children". They don't call us that.

Character-building

GNVQ is much more student-led than
A-levels are, so you have to initiate things
yourself and learn how to relate to people.
Working independently makes you more self-
confident. I'm much more self-confident than
I was last year.

Co-operation

I like the fact that a lot of people are involved
and everyone helps each other. If you have a
problem, you can talk to people on the same
programme. And the teachers are
approachable. They don't just talk at you, with
you listening.

5 Looking at the Alternatives

This chapter runs through the other options that may be available to you.

They include:

- employment
- AS and GCE A-levels
- National Vocational Qualifications (NVQs)
- Modern Apprenticeships
- other vocational qualifications.

When considering your range of options, bear in mind that GNVQs bridge the gap between purely academic and vocational qualifications, allowing you to transfer to one or the other at the appropriate level.

Because GNVQs are relatively new, the chances are you will want to consider other, tried and tested courses. The important thing is that the course you decide on is relevant and attainable. There's no point chasing a qualification just because it's highly regarded by universities. Nor is it always in your best interests to sign up for a vocational course because it appears to offer the shortest route to the job you want.

Employment

You can, of course, leave school straight for a job. The immediate attractions are plain:

- you'll be paid for your work
- employment will give you a measure of independence
- any training you receive will be relevant to your work.

But going straight into employment at 16 may not be your best move, especially in the long term. Drawbacks include:

➡ your starting position and salary will be relatively low
➡ your lack of qualifications may harm your promotion prospects
➡ if you decide that your first job isn't right for you, your lack of qualifications may make it difficult to find other work.

A lot will depend on what jobs are open to you. Some employers actually prefer to take on school-leavers and train them in the workplace. If you have decent GCSEs and have been offered a secure job with proper training, the prospect is worth considering. Otherwise, think hard before taking the plunge. Few jobs are for life, and a lack of qualifications at 16 could seriously affect future employment prospects. Even if you find secure employment, you may discover that, without qualifications, you get passed over for promotion. It would be a bitter experience to find that new employees who have stayed on at school or college are promoted over you.

At the least, consider staying on in further education for a one-year full-time, or a two-year part-time, vocational course, perhaps combined with additional GCSEs, or resits in maths and English. Alternatively, you could take an NVQ, the workplace equivalent of GNVQs.

From September 1995, many employers in a wide range of sectors will be offering Modern Apprenticeships to school-leavers in the 16 to 17 age range. These programmes, which are explained on page 135, offer genuine work-based training and qualifications to entrants with little or no previous vocational education. They can also offer a clear vocational progression route for students who might have completed a Foundation or Intermediate GNVQ.

AS and GCE A-levels

If you have a minimum of four GCSEs at A–C, then you are probably in a position to choose either Advanced GNVQs or GCE A-levels, *or* a combination of the two.

GCE A-levels have several plus points. The qualifications:

❥ are familiar and universally recognised
❥ are offered in hundreds of subjects
❥ develop a detailed knowledge of a particular subject(s)
❥ meet entry requirements for higher education and professional courses.

It should also be added that GCE A-levels:

❥ do not suit all students
❥ are narrow in scope
❥ do not provide much in the way of training for a job, or preparation for employment in general
❥ give you only one chance to succeed – the end-of-course exams.

GCE A-levels are now offered in nearly 400 syllabuses, from accounting and ancient history to woodwork and zoology. In 1994 there were about three-quarters of a million GCE A-level entries. Most students take two or three complementary GCE A-levels – maths, physics and chemistry, for example – or English, history and a foreign language – but combining unrelated subjects is becoming more common and more widely accepted as entry qualifications for higher education.

AS courses were introduced to give GCE A-level students the chance to broaden their studies and increase their options. Like GCE A-levels, they are two-year courses, but they cover only half a GCE A-level syllabus, thus allowing, say, a science student to keep a language or to add a different subject.

AS and GCE A-levels are equally demanding, and much more intensive than GCSE courses. Whatever your chosen subject, you will need to read widely and in depth. You will have to analyse, form judgments and express them in writing – usually in the form of essays. Some syllabuses include orals, projects or other practical work, which are marked or assessed, but your final result will be largely determined by how well you do in the end-of-course examinations.

Two GCE A-levels with good grades is usually the minimum requirement for entry to a degree course. Most GCE A-level students take three. Two AS courses are generally accepted in place of one GCE A-level. Some popular and specialist degree courses – English and medicine, for example – will be out of reach unless you have three good GCE A-levels in the right subjects. One GCE A-level is not enough in itself to win entry to a degree course, although it may be sufficient (if supported by the right GCSEs) to get you on to a higher vocational programme that offers progression to a degree course.

GCE A-levels are also accepted for entry to professional and semi-professional bodies. Two GCE A-levels or equivalent will get you on to courses in accountancy, advertising, hotel catering, occupational therapy, physiotherapy, and surveying.

Because GCE A-levels open so many doors, you might not give a second thought to other qualifications. But it's worth taking a moment to consider two important implications of an all-GCE A-level programme:

- ➡ you will develop academic expertise in your chosen subjects, but few of the practical skills and knowledge that are required in the world of work
- ➡ the high rewards GCE A-levels can bring are matched by risks. If you fail the exams or obtain poor grades, you may end up with little or nothing to show for two years' efforts.

Is a GNVQ for Me?

The following piece is by Jane Harrop. Jane is Head of GNVQ Implementation at NCVQ. The GNVQ unit co-ordinates the development and evaluation of GNVQs in schools and colleges and consults regularly with employers, teachers and other professional groups.

Would I enjoy GNVQ-type study as opposed to that offered by AS/GCE A-levels or other vocational qualifications?

Do you like discussing things with other people, working in a group, getting out and talking to people about their jobs? Do you like making decisions about what sort of projects you want to do, how to carry them out, creating opportunities to get information, and sharing it with others in various ways? With GNVQs there are plenty of different things to do, mostly in projects YOU plan with your teacher or in a group, and you will decide how best to do them.

You will have to write up your projects, and will often be asked to give your own opinion and evaluation of what you have investigated, as well as reporting what others do and think. You will have to ask a lot of questions, so you will become good at different types of research: interviewing people, looking at the environment in which people live and work, both economic and physical, finding information, reading newspapers, as well as using textbooks.

Everyone has to do some word-processing, graphics and spreadsheet work, as so many people do now in their jobs. You will use some maths to help illustrate your work, whether it's to show the financial picture, explain the statistical importance of your research, or solve problems if you are doing a science-related subject.

You won't spend all your time sitting at a desk studying on your own; more likely you'll be finding out how a hospital works, organising a school/college event or meeting, producing marketing materials, setting up and running experiments, deciding where and why to put up a building, and proposing valuable ideas on how to improve someone's business. Sometimes you may actually take part in a business or simulation to complete a project. Most of what you do is about present day events, but you'll also look at why things have changed and may change in the future.

What would be the value of this qualification as opposed to others?

GNVQs are still new but people are getting to know that they have a recognised national status, just like GCE A-levels or GCSEs. Each level of GNVQ shows that you have reached a particular standard of intellectual development. The Advanced GNVQ is similar to taking at least two GCE A-levels and each one covers a broad range of studies under one title. The Intermediate GNVQ, including the core skills, is equivalent to four to five GCSEs at grades A–C. This can be a preparation for the Advanced GNVQ or other courses. You may find that you also need particular GCSEs, such as English or maths, to move on to certain courses. The Foundation GNVQs have the same breadth of study but are easier than Intermediate and count as four to five GCSEs at grades D–F. GNVQ graduates are well-informed individuals, good communicators and used to working with others, as well as alone. Most employers and people in higher education think those skills are very useful for work and further study. But you may need to explain to people exactly what you have done during your GNVQ course, and show how your particular knowledge and skills match what they need, with examples from your project work. People have an idea what different academic subjects are, and you may have to tell them what subjects you have combined in your GNVQ. For instance, Business includes some economics, finance, law and management. Health and Social Care includes some nutrition and hygiene, human biology, social policy and social research.

Where would a GNVQ lead as opposed to other qualifications?

When you look in more detail at GNVQs or GCE A-levels each can lead in different directions. If you have some ideas about what you want to do next you need to find out what GNVQs or other qualifications are required. For some jobs, an employer will say 'I want someone who knows about what we do already, is interested and understands it, and so is likely to become quickly involved. A GNVQ does that, rather than GCE A-levels.' Employers should not expect you to have all the skills you need for a job already; many jobs give opportunities to learn these by doing an NVQ.

Some university courses will be very interested in the different aspects you have included in your GNVQ, for instance, some basic physics, maths and design in the Manufacturing GNVQ, or some economics, geography and human resource management for Leisure and Tourism. Foundation and Intermediate GNVQs give you a choice of moving on to a higher level GNVQ or an appropriate NVQ. However, if you are really interested in certain GCE A-levels and know that you want to do the same thing but more at university, then you should probably not do a GNVQ.

GCE A-level reforms

If you have decided that GCE A-levels are definitely not for you, you may have to think again. By the time you enter further education, you may find that the differences between GNVQs and certain GCE A-levels are not so great as you might think.

In 1993 the examination boards were given the go-ahead to introduce AS and GCE A-level syllabuses containing up to six modules – self-contained units, rather like the units in GNVQs. Under the new proposals, you would still take an end-of-course examination covering the whole syllabus, but a much greater percentage of marks can come from unit tests taken during the course.

Passes in some modules in certain GCE A-levels might also count as credits towards an Advanced GNVQ. For example, you might take some maths modules as units in Advanced Science or Manufacturing GNVQs. This linkage between the two qualifications could mean that it would be possible for you to take some common modules before committing yourself to a full GCE A-level course or to a GNVQ programme.

Another significant feature is the number of modules. Six, of course, is the number of GNVQ units considered the equivalent of one A-level. By designing A-levels with the same number of modules, the awarding bodies are making the equivalence plain.

Not all GCE A-levels will lend themselves to a modular structure. But for GCE A-level subjects that have a direct relation to work – sciences, engineering, social sciences and business – it does seem that modular versions will be available soon.

National Vocational Qualifications

NVQs are the workplace equivalents of GNVQs. They develop actual *work skills*. If you want proper vocational training on the job, then these may be the most suitable qualifications for you.

Here are the good points of NVQs. They:

- cover a very wide range of occupations
- are offered at different levels
- allow natural progression up the levels
- are widely recognised and valued by employers.

And here is the chief drawback of NVQs:

➤ Most of them are available only to people in work, or with regular access to the workplace.

No matter what area of work you are interested in, there is probably an NVQ that covers it. Although they are relatively new qualifications, there are already more than 300 NVQs, in occupations as diverse as fish husbandry and scientific glass blowing. Together with GNVQs, they are intended to become the main national qualification in vocational education, with half the workforce aiming for NVQs by 1996.

As their name suggests, NVQs have similarities with GNVQs. The most important distinction is that NVQs must be assessed in the workplace, but there are other differences, as you will see from the following comparison:

NVQs are offered at a range of levels, with level 1 representing basic skills. At present, four levels are in place, but a fifth level is planned. The three lower levels correspond with the GNVQ levels, and there is also equivalence with other qualifications, including GCSEs and GCE A-levels, as shown in the proposed National Framework of Qualifications on page 13.

Comparative features of GNVQs and NVQs		
	GNVQs	NVQs
Aimed at	full-time students	mainly employees and some students
Develop	general vocational skills and understanding	occupational competence
Assessed	mainly outside workplace	in workplace or simulated workplace
Standards developed by	NCVQ and awarding bodies	employers
Titles available	limited number in each vocational area	wide number in each occupational area

The TECs are the local experts on NVQs. They work closely with employers who support NVQs and they will be able to tell you exactly what NVQ opportunities are available in your area. They can also advise you where to obtain information from the NVQ national database, which tells you not only what NVQs are currently available, but also what units are required and how each unit is made up.

Where can I find out more?

➡ your school, college or careers guidance centre
➡ your nearest Training and Enterprise Council (TEC)
➡ the NVQ-awarding bodies and NCVQ.

Other sources of information about NVQs are the NVQ-awarding bodies. There are several dozen of these, but the major bodies are BTEC, City and Guilds, and RSA, which are also the awarding bodies for GNVQs. Their addresses and telephone numbers are given at the end of this chapter, together with the address of the National Council for Vocational Qualifications (NCVQ), the body which approves the standards for both NVQs and GNVQs.

Combining GNVQ and NVQ units

Research indicates that it should be feasible for students to combine units from GNVQs and NVQs. For students on GNVQ programmes, additional NVQ units would bring:

- the opportunity to learn occupational skills in a realistic work environment, through work placements and exposure to NVQ assessment methods
- additional qualifications, in the form of NVQ units or credits towards them
- improved employment prospects.

For people working towards NVQs with college support, GNVQs would provide:

- added value through achieving credits in core skills units, which at present are not included in NVQs
- a way of gaining knowledge and understanding of skills relevant to a whole vocational area.

Modern Apprenticeships

A combination of GNVQ and NVQ units is likely to be part of the programme followed by trainees in the government-backed Modern Apprenticeship scheme, which will start in September 1995. Designed and developed by employers and Industry Training Organisations (ITOs) in conjunction with TECs, Modern Apprenticeships offer school-leavers training leading to an NVQ at level 3 or above. By the end of this decade an estimated 150,000 young people will be in Modern Apprenticeship training and 40,000 will graduate each year from the scheme with NVQ level 3 or above.

Individual employers and sectors will develop their own Modern Apprenticeship models, but they will be based on a framework of common features to ensure consistency and quality. The common features cover:

- **Eligibility:** The normal age range for trainees will be 16 to 17, although slightly older entrants won't necessarily be ruled out. Employers will recommend the selection requirements, but will be aware that academic achievement is not the only measure of potential.
- **Training content and outcome:** The sector will make clear the skills, knowledge and understanding the apprentice is to develop. This training must lead to an NVQ at level 3 or above. It might include core skills, supervisory skills and/or entrepreneurial skills, drawing on units from related GNVQs or NVQs.
- **Timescale:** Training outcomes must be achieved in the shortest possible timescale (an average of three years).
- **Training contract and status:** The training plan will be set out in a contract between the employer and the trainee. Ideally, all trainees should have employed status while training. Wages will be a matter between the trainee and the employer, but they should reflect the trainee's achievement on the course.

Fourteen employment sectors have been involved in developing Modern Apprenticeships:

- Agriculture and Commercial Horticulture
- Business Administration
- Chemicals Industry
- Child Care
- Electrical Installation Engineering
- Engineering Construction Sector
- Engineering Manufacturing Sector
- Information Technology
- Marine Engineering
- Merchant Navy
- Polymers Sector
- Retailing
- Steel Industry
- Travel Services.

Around 40 sectors and ITOs – from the Booksellers' Association to the Confederation of British Wool Textiles – have said that they are interested in starting Modern Apprenticeships from 1995.

IMPORTANT!

- Modern Apprenticeships are not available in Scotland and will only be available in Wales in the Engineering sector.

To give you an idea of how a Modern Apprenticeship would work, here is a prototype scheme developed for Engineering Manufacturing. An apprenticeship leading to NVQ level 3 would consist of:

- work-based training to acquire the NVQ level 3 competences
- an appropriate programme of vocational education delivered in an approved centre (eg a school, a college or an employer's training centre). The vocational

education part of the programme is likely to be provided by existing qualifications, including GNVQ core skills and vocational units. These would provide:

- a contribution to the acquisition of core skills
- some of the underpinning knowledge and understanding required for NVQ levels 3 and 4
- other broader knowledge and understanding required as a basis for further progression and career development.

Trainees could enter such a scheme with little or no vocational education, but entrants with Foundation or Intermediate GNVQ would probably be credited for prior achievements and would complete their apprenticeship in a shorter time.

Modern Apprenticeships are still being developed and refined. To find out more, contact your local TEC or careers office.

Other vocational qualifications

There are literally hundreds of different vocational courses, but only a limited number are available nationally to full-time further education students. Some of these correspond to GNVQs and will be phased out as the new qualifications are introduced. Even in the first year of GNVQs, some students transferred to the new programmes from other vocational courses.

Most of the vocational qualifications for 16- to 19-year-olds are offered by the three organisations that award GNVQs:

- BTEC
- City and Guilds
- RSA.

BTEC awards First and National Qualifications. These:

➻ are offered in dozens of courses covering the same broad vocational areas as GNVQs
➻ can be taken as a one-year, part-time course leading to a First Certificate or as a one-year, full-time or two-year, part-time course leading to a First Diploma.

City and Guilds offers the Diploma of Vocational Education in many vocational fields at Intermediate level and National level. Some of them cover the same areas as GNVQs and, where there is overlap, the older qualification will be phased out.

IMPORTANT!

➻ Bear in mind that many First and National Qualifications will be phased out as the corresponding GNVQs become generally available.

RSA, the other GNVQ-awarding body, offers other vocational courses in the fields of:

➻ business
➻ financial services
➻ information technology
➻ languages
➻ office skills
➻ manufacturing
➻ retailing
➻ wholesaling
➻ warehousing.

RSA is also developing a new range of vocational GCSEs in design and technology, information technology and languages. These will satisfy the requirements of the National Curriculum, but will be related to the world of work.

Where can I find out more?

→ **BTEC**
Central House
Upper Woburn Place
London WC1H 0HH
Tel: 0171-413 8400

→ **City and Guilds of London Institute**
46 Britannia Street
London WC1X 9RG
Tel: 0171-278 2468

→ **RSA Examinations Board**
Westwood Way
Coventry CV4 8HS
Tel: 01203 470033

→ **National Council for Vocational Qualifications**
222 Euston Road
London NW1 2BZ
Tel: 0171-387 9898

For more general advice, speak to your local careers guidance experts – either at their centre or during their visits to your school. They are well informed about all the available options, including GNVQs, and they will explain the advantages and disadvantages of each, without putting you under pressure to make a particular choice.

At one school, a visiting careers guide talked to a student who wanted to gain qualifications for a career in health and social care. The student was planning to take GCE A-levels, but she wasn't sure what subjects would be most appropriate. Also, she was a bit worried about the risk of failing. She hadn't heard of GNVQs, but when the careers guide explained how they worked and told her about the GNVQ in Health and Social Care, 'her eyes lit up'. Here was a package covering all her interests and abilities.

'After that,' said the careers guide, 'I have no doubts that GNVQs will prove a real blessing to many students.'

Combining GNVQs with other qualifications

Remember that enrolling for a GNVQ doesn't rule out other options. Most students are taking GNVQs as part of a package that also includes GCSEs, GCE A-levels or other vocational qualifications. In fact, for most purposes, it's wrong to think of GNVQs as alternatives to other qualifications; they will slot neatly in with many other courses.

Another option favoured by some centres is to offer students additional GNVQ units, which tend to be occupation-specific or geared to students aiming for higher education. At centres offering additional units, you will usually be given the chance to take six with an Advanced GNVQ. The reasoning behind this is that since the Advanced GNVQ (which has 12 vocational units) is deemed to be of a standard comparable with two GCE A-levels, six additional units are equivalent to one GCE A-level. Unlike optional units, additional units can be chosen from different vocational areas.

General Scottish Vocational Qualifications

GSVQ is the best shape that National
Certificate has ever taken. It's a family of
related skills which takes a student to a
reasonably competent level. It lets them get
into the job market and it's a path to further
and higher education that is ideal for
everyone.

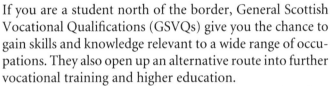

A GSVQ tutor

If you are a student north of the border, General Scottish
Vocational Qualifications (GSVQs) give you the chance to
gain skills and knowledge relevant to a wide range of occupations. They also open up an alternative route into further
vocational training and higher education.

Although they are new qualifications, introduced in
1992, GSVQs are based on the familiar National Certificate
Modules. They are qualifications in their own right, but you
can combine a GSVQ programme with other courses,
including additional National Certificate Modules or, timetable permitting, Highers. A tutor at a college offering level
II explains:

We've designed a programme that includes
more than the GSVQ. We build in a lot of
modules that we feel are of benefit to students
either going into the workplace or higher level
courses.

As their name suggests, GSVQs have links with SVQs, the
occupational awards. Both qualifications are assessment-
based and are designed to enable students to build up

credits towards the full award. Unlike SVQs, however, GSVQs are not assessed in the workplace.

GSVQs also have similarities with GNVQs, the general vocational qualification available to students elsewhere in the UK. GSVQs, however, have been developed from proven Scottish vocational qualifications. They are administered by the Scottish Vocational Education Council (SCOTVEC), which is also the awarding body for occupational SVQs, and Higher National Certificates (HNCs), Higher National Diplomas (HNDs) and other vocational qualifications in Scotland.

Because GSVQs fit into a framework of established vocational qualifications administered by the same awarding body, they will be of particular interest to students who plan to take further vocational training, either in the workplace or college.

Educational reforms and GSVQs

Despite the high regard in which Scottish education is held – on both sides of the border – there has been a debate about how it can be improved to meet the needs and challenges of the future. In 1990, a committee chaired by Professor John Howie was appointed by the government to identify the weaknesses of the system and build on its strengths.

The government's detailed response to the recommendations of the Howie Report is given in the publication *Higher Still: Opportunities for All*, available from the Scottish Office Publications Sale, 1/44 New St Andrew's House, St James Centre, Edinburgh EH1 3TG (tel: 0131-556 8400) (price £2.00). The response reflects the government's wish to create a twin-track system, with academic and vocational courses having equal status. Among the main changes to be introduced from 1997 are:

- Scottish Education Board (SEB) and SCOTVEC

courses, including GSVQ, will be brought into a unified curriculum and assessment system
- ➤➤ new curriculum guidelines will be developed to allow students to demonstrate proficiency in the core skills of Communication, Numeracy, Information Technology, Personal and Interpersonal Skills, and Problem-solving. The report points out that core skills are an important feature of GSVQs
- ➤➤ Highers will remain, and Advanced Highers will be developed to provide challenging two-year courses. Both courses will have a modular structure, as in GSVQs.

As *Higher Still* makes clear:

> The Higher and Advanced Higher courses will be modular in structure and drawn from current SEB and SCOTVEC provision, so that students are able to study "vocational" as well as "academic" courses at demanding levels. The distinction between "academic" and "vocational" education is in many ways a false one. So-called academic courses often develop knowledge and skills which are highly relevant in employment; while well-designed "vocational" courses must include the development of knowledge and understanding. Students should be able to take a mix of courses as best suits their aptitudes and aspirations. Highers and Advanced Highers based on current SCOTVEC provision will be created by adapting, developing and bringing together into coherent clusters existing National Certificate modules and Higher National units at the appropriate level.

Recognising the need to prepare for the changes through a comprehensive development programme, the government plans to introduce the new system from the 1997–98 session.

Programmes available

GSVQs are offered in the broad vocational areas:

- Arts and Social Sciences
- Business Administration
- Care
- Design
- Hospitality
- Information Technology
- Land-based Industries
- Leisure and Tourism
- Science
- Technology.

The range of levels

GSVQs are aimed mainly at 16- to 19-year-olds, but they may also be suitable for adults who want a qualification that will improve their employment prospects, or who are planning a change of career. Depending on your abilities and previous qualifications, you can take a GSVQ at one of three levels – from I to III. The higher the level, the more demanding the programme:

- level I is a general qualification which covers basic skills and knowledge relevant to a range of vocational areas
- levels II and III are designed to develop skills, knowledge and understanding relating to a particular vocational area.

If you are a slow learner or lack formal qualifications, you can still get a foot on the ladder by taking one of the two preliminary awards – Skillstart 1 and Skillstart 2 – which offer progression to GSVQs.

NB: All GSVQs at a particular level have the same number of credits.

Skillstart 1 consists of six credits and is suitable for students with moderate learning difficulties. The programme will normally take one year.

Skillstart 2 consists of nine credits, of which three are common to both Skillstart awards. This programme usually takes one year and is suitable for full-time students and for adults who lack formal qualifications and who want a qualification that will help improve their employment prospects. Alternatively, a student gaining this award can go on to take a GSVQ.

Level I GSVQ consists of 12 credits. Because it is not linked to any particular vocational area, this programme is suitable for students who have not decided what occupation they wish to follow, or who lack the qualifications needed for entry to levels II and III. Programmes normally take one year. Although there are no pre-entry requirements for this award, you might need relevant qualifications to take some modules.

When you have gained level I, you can go on to take a GSVQ at a higher level. Another option would be to take an occupational SVQ in a particular vocational area.

Level II GSVQ consists of 12 credits in one of the ten vocational areas. Programmes will normally take one year. Although there are no formal entry requirements for these awards, you would typically be expected to have one of the following:

- an award at level I GSVQ
- passes in between eight and ten relevant National Certificate Modules
- four relevant passes at Standard Grade level 3 or at Ordinary Grade, including English.

If you gain an award at this level, various routes are open to you. You could go on to:

➤ a level III programme in the same or a different vocational area

➤ an occupational SVQ

➤ various Scottish Wider Access Programmes.

Level III GSVQ consists of 18 credits in one of the ten vocational areas. Programmes will normally take two years. Although there are no formal entry requirements for these awards, you would typically be expected to have one of the following:

➤ an award in a relevant level II GSVQ

➤ at least four relevant passes at Standard Grade level 2/3 or Ordinary Grade, including English

➤ relevant passes at Higher Grade (for mature students).

If you gain a GSVQ at this level, various routes are open. They include:

➤ administrative posts in a number of organisations that recognise the value of GSVQs

➤ Higher National Certificates (HNCs)

➤ Higher National Diplomas (HNDs)

➤ degree courses

➤ teacher training.

National Certificate Modules

GSVQs are based on National Certificate Modules, which are already familiar to many students in Scottish schools and colleges.

Students shouldn't have any problems understanding the new qualification, because many of the modules included in GSVQs were already part of their programme.

A college lecturer

'The problem with old National Certificate programmes', a GSVQ tutor explained, 'is that they were too wide-ranging, too confusing for employers. SVQs are fine, but they're narrow and they have to be assessed in the workplace. GSVQs are an ideal compromise – coherent, relevant, ideal for students in full-time education.'

Each GSVQ is a package of National Certificate Modules that have been grouped to cover the skills and knowledge relevant to a broad vocational area. In designing module groupings that meet the standards required by employers, higher education institutions and other organisations, SCOTVEC consulted extensively with experts in the educational and occupational sectors.

For each module you achieve, you'll be given a credit. Most modules are worth one credit. A credit is a mini-qualification in its own right and also counts towards the award of the full GSVQ. As a rough guide, it should take about 40 hours of study to achieve one module.

How a National Certificate Module works

Modules tell you:

- ◆▸ what area of competence you will be working in (see chapter 1, page 24, for more information about the term 'area of competence')
- ◆▸ what you have to do to prove your competence
- ◆▸ how the evidence of your competence should be presented.

The best way to understand the requirements of a GSVQ programme is to break down an actual module into its various parts. The following example, 'Housing administration 1', is one of the optional modules in level III Business Administration.

Module title

Each module has a number and a title:

- ◆→ the number 82507 identifies, for example, the module 'Housing administration 1' and avoids any confusion with other modules covering the same area, such as 'Housing administration 2'
- ◆→ the title tells you what area of competence you'll be working in.

Credit value

Each module in a GSVQ programme has a credit value that counts towards the full award. The value of each module is given in the overall specifications (see 'Unit specifications' in the glossary of terms) for each programme. In level III Business Administration, 'Housing administration 1' counts as one credit towards the 18 credits needed for the full award.

Purpose

The following example tells you more about the area of competence covered by the module and outlines the skills and knowledge that you will develop.

'Housing administration 1' is described as an initial module in housing administration for those interested or employed in all sectors of housing, eg housing authorities, pressure groups, estate agents, etc. This module will develop an understanding of how housing has developed, the various methods of provision, and the roles and re-sponsibilities of housing providers.

Preferred entry level

To tackle some modules successfully, you may need relevant previous qualifications or experience. For 'Housing administration 1', it is recommended that you have a credit in Communication level 3, one of the National Certificate core skills modules, or a Standard Grade in English at level 3.

Outcomes

In order to gain a credit in 'Housing administration 1', you should:

•→ understand the factors that have influenced current housing provision
•→ understand the nature of the housing market and the methods of access to the various types of housing
•→ analyse housing problems with reference to current legislation.

Performance criteria

Performance criteria spell out what you *must* do to achieve each outcome. For Outcome 2, 'Understand the nature of the housing market', you must meet all the following performance criteria:

•→ outline the types of housing available in the community
•→ contrast relative proportions of various types of housing available in the local area, with national figures
•→ describe methods of access to each available type of housing
•→ state the standard criteria for access to each type of housing.

Range statements

Many modules include range statements. These set limits around the skills and knowledge that you will be expected to demonstrate. The 'Housing administration' module doesn't include range statements, but it does give information that will help you fully understand the performance criteria. For example, it explains that the different types of housing provision referred to above cover private ownership, private-rented, public-rented and housing associations.

Assignments and projects

To meet the performance criteria, you have to produce relevant evidence. This evidence will come from projects and assignments tailored to fit the requirements of each outcome. Your assignments will usually be set by tutors, working from guidelines set out in the modules.

For example, to demonstrate satisfactory performance in Outcome 2 of the 'Housing administration' module, you may be asked to produce a report of about 800 words that:

- identifies the range of housing types locally
- estimates the proportion of available types and compares it with national figures
- lists the methods of access to each type
- lists the standard criteria for access to each type.

This assignment may involve obtaining information from local housing authorities, building societies, election rolls, etc.

Wherever possible, tutors will try to devise assignments that simulate workplace tasks in your vocational area. For example, you might be expected to act the part of an employee doing a particular task, with your teacher playing the role of supervisor. Your programme will also involve out-of-school links and activities.

As a college tutor explains:

If it's appropriate we get guest speakers in. Or we'll take the students on visits. Some modules encourage out-of-school projects. In Problem-solving, for example, the students might go into building societies and finance companies to find out about interest rates and compare different ways of borrowing. If the module lends itself to it, we encourage the students to get out because it develops their independence. But a lot of the modules in GSVQs are more classroom-based, and because they're precise in their requirements, there's not always the opportunity to let the students do something different. However, recently things have become more flexible and centres can exercise some discretion in their delivery and assessment.

Some of your assignments will be aimed at tackling outcomes from more than one module.

Work experience

At many GSVQ centres, work experience is considered an important part of the programme, developing actual competence in occupational tasks. A college tutor explains how work experience is built into the level II Business Administration programme at his college: 'We work in blocks of 13 weeks. Normally for one block the students go out on work experience for either one full day or one morning and one afternoon a week. The course tutor sets up the work placement and decides where the student goes.'

Guidance

GSVQ students are encouraged to show personal initiative, but you will be given advice and encouragement at all stages of your programme.

A level II Business Administration tutor explained that some of her students 'found it a bit different from what they were used to, but once they got into it they really did enjoy it. We made sure that they had all the facilities they required and access to all the tutors in individual subjects if they needed any help or guidance. And then there was a lecturer – in this case myself – who was in class to give them guidance about the projects. They did really well. All of them passed, and four in my group got Merit.'

Assessment

At regular intervals your teachers will assess your work to see if it meets the requirements set out in the modules. They will examine your work to see if you have:

- ➡ achieved the module outcomes
- ➡ met all the performance criteria
- ➡ satisfied all the range statements
- ➡ produced the evidence in the form required – report, survey, case-study, etc.

Core skills

All GSVQ programmes include five compulsory core skills which will be useful in any walk of life.

1 **Communication** is the ability to write and talk appropriately for a particular purpose and audience, and to understand and interpret information through reading and listening.
2 **Numeracy** is the ability to use a range of arithmetical and basic statistical techniques to reach conclusions in practical situations.
3 **Information Technology** is the ability to use computers to sort, process and retrieve information and to present information in forms appropriate to a particular purpose and audience.
4 **Personal and Interpersonal Skills** are the ability to work independently and co-operatively with others, and to use self-awareness and social awareness to guide action.
5 **Problem-solving** is the ability to identify and evaluate problems and to devise ways to solve them.

Each of the core skills has been specified at four stages of difficulty, from 1 to 4. GSVQs include all five core skills, but the stage of difficulty you must achieve for each skill varies according to how important it is to your vocational area. For example, in Arts and Social Sciences, where Communication skills are particularly important, level III students must achieve Communication at stage 4 and Numeracy at stage 2. By contrast, in Technology, where Numeracy is a vital skill, level III students must achieve both Communication at stage 3 and Numeracy at stage 3.

Skills in Communication, Numeracy and Information Technology are assessed through special core skills modules. Standard grades in English and maths are, however, accepted in place of core skills in Communication and Numeracy. Personal and Interpersonal Skills and Problem-solving may be included in vocational modules. For example, in level III Technology, Problem-solving skills are built into the module 'Applied technology', while in level III Care, Personal and Interpersonal Skills are built into a module called 'Practical caring skills'.

Skillstart programmes include special starter stage core skills or higher.

Specifications for GSVQs and Skillstart

The following details will give you a general idea of the range of modules covered by GSVQs at the different levels and the two stages of Skillstart.

Skillstart 1

Core skills
Three credits, one from each of the following mandatory modules:

- Skillstart communication
- personal organisation
- using numbers in everyday situations.

Work-related modules
One credit from one of the following modules:

- Skillstart investigation: the world of work
- finding and keeping a job

- Skillstart enterprise activity
- introduction to working with people
- introduction to working with tools.

Optional modules
Two credits chosen from the following modules:

- the building industry
- warehouse practice
- the manufacturing industry
- land industries
- auto-engineering
- catering (food preparation)
- catering (food service)
- office practice
- an appreciation of retail
- working with children
- working with the elderly.

Skillstart 2

Core skills
Three credits, one from each of the following modules:

- Skillstart communication
- Skillstart investigation: the world of work
- using numbers in everyday situations.

One credit in one of the following modules:

- local investigations
- work experience
- residential experience
- experiencing Europe
- investigating Europe
- contemporary issues.

Work-related modules
Two credits chosen from the following modules:

- information technology
- job-seeking skills
- Skillstart enterprise activity

- introduction to working with people
- introduction to working with tools
- organisation of practical skills
- accident and emergency procedures.

Optional modules
Three credits from one of the nine following groups:

- office practice
- horticulture
- agriculture
- retail
- manufacturing industry
- building industry A (focusing on trowel skills and interior finishes)
- building industry B (focusing mainly on carpentry and joinery)
- auto-engineering
- catering (food preparation).

Level I GSVQ

Core skills
Five credits.

Mandatory modules
One credit from any of the following work-related modules:

- job-seeking skills
- enterprise activity
- community involvement
- life and work
- personal effectiveness
- work-shadowing
- roles and behaviour.

Optional modules
Six credits – three credits from each of two of the following groups:

➻ office practice (covers keyboard skills, office work, working in a reception area, text-processing)

➻ horticulture (tree and shrub planting, using horticultural hand tools, basic gardening skills, bedding plant production)

➻ agriculture (basic care of mammals, tractor operation, estate maintenance, farm building maintenance, land-based production)

➻ retail (basic retail skills, customer contact, selling skills, display)

➻ manufacturing industry (design and make, engineering workshop practice, assembly skills, machinery maintenance, marking-out procedures, graphical engineering communication)

➻ building industry A (focusing on trowel skills and interior finishes)

➻ building industry B (focusing on carpentry and joinery)

➻ auto-engineering (covers use and care of motor vehicle tools and workshop equipment, vehicle layout, vehicle electrical systems, vehicle securing and sealing devices, fitting, fault diagnosis and repairs of wheels, tyres and exhaust systems

➻ catering (food preparation, cookery processes, meal production, food preparation techniques)

➻ technology (mechanics, electricity, core mathematics)

➻ electrical and electronic systems (design and make, introduction to electronic and electrical systems, practical science skills, instrumentation and measurement techniques)

➻ computing in manufacture (computer-aided manufacture, computer application packages, computing in engineering)

➻ construction (building craft science, basic building mechanics, construction crafts technology, construction procedures)

- information technology (computer hardware, software, application packages)
- home economics (food preparation and cookery skills, fabric crafts, hygiene, home safety and health of children and young people)
- Europe (includes all major European languages, as well as investigating and experiencing Europe).

Level II Arts and Social Sciences

Core skills
Five credits.

Mandatory modules
Three credits including:

- introduction to literature
- information skills
- learning skills
- introduction to people and society.

Optional modules
Four credits from two of the following groups – two from each:

- social subjects (people and the past; people and politics; people and the environment; people and society)
- languages (a choice of European languages, plus the option of English as a foreign language)
- history of art (seven modules covering the history of art from c. 4000 BC to c. AD 1960)
- creative and aesthetic (creative drama, history of theatre, listening to music, general media studies, creative writing)
- additional (a broad range of modules covering

religion, law, economics, psychology, philosophy and mathematics).

A pass in the additional assessment is also required.

Level III Arts and Social Sciences

Core skills
Six credits.

Mandatory modules
Three credits covering:

- writing papers and reports
- literature
- information skills
- learning skills.

Optional modules
Nine credits from three of the following groups – three from each:

- history
- politics
- sociology
- geography
- religious studies
- philosophy
- psychology
- languages
- additional (a broad range of modules, including media studies, European Community processes, economic issues, oral presentation skills, creative writing and mathematics).

A pass in the additional assessment is also required.

Level II Business Administration

Core skills
Five credits.

Mandatory modules
One credit from each of these:

- ◆ financial record-keeping
- ◆ working in an office
- ◆ economics of the market
- ◆ the Scottish legal framework.

Optional modules
Three credits from a range of more than 20 modules, covering areas in:

- ◆ accounting
- ◆ word processing
- ◆ consumer studies
- ◆ purchasing principles
- ◆ European issues
- ◆ European languages.

A pass in the additional assessment is also required.

Level III Business Administration

Core skills
Six credits.

Mandatory modules
One credit from each of the following:

- ◆ introduction to office management
- ◆ basic applications of behavioural science
- ◆ contemporary macro-economic issues
- ◆ contract law
- ◆ introduction to marketing
- ◆ financial record-keeping.

Optional modules

Six credits from a range of more than 25 modules covering areas in:

- accounting
- computer applications
- housing
- tourist attractions and services
- local government and law.

A pass in the additional assessment is also required.

Level II Care

Core skills
Six credits.

Mandatory modules
Three credits.

Modules cover accident and emergency procedures, human development and promoting equal opportunities.

Optional modules
Three credits.

The options cover the general field of care, and include modules in care provision for children and the elderly, health promotion, nutrition, the work environment, mental health issues and practical science skills.

A pass in the additional assessment is also required.

Level III Care

Core skills
Seven credits.

Mandatory modules
Three credits.

The modules cover first-aid, human behaviour and stressful situations.

Optional modules
Eight credits.

These modules look at particular aspects of care, as well as general issues. They include welfare provision in Scotland, budgeting and finance for care, puberty, counselling, care for children under eight, promoting equal opportunities, and causes and prevention of disease.

A pass in the additional assessment is also required.

Level II Design

Core skills
Four credits.

Mandatory modules
Six credits.

These modules provide an introduction to various aspects of design, including 2-D and 3-D design, and drawing skills.

Optional modules
Two credits.

The options allow students to extend the skills covered in the mandatory modules, and also offer the opportunity to learn about particular design skills in various fields, including ceramics, fabrics, photography, fashion and video production.

A pass in the additional assessment is also required.

Level III Design

Core skills
Four credits.

Mandatory modules

Three credits, one from each of the following:

- design in context
- design realisation
- design in action.

Optional modules

A total of 11 credits, to be gained as follows:

- Two credits from a general group of modules covering colour, film animation, history of art, computer-aided draughting and stained glass techniques.
- Nine credits – three credits from each of three of the following groups:

drawing	ceramics and pottery
fine art	fabric and textile crafts
illustration	fashion design
graphic design	photography
letterforms	audio visual
product design	engineering design
spatial design	print-making.
jewellery design	

A pass in the additional assessment is also required.

Level II Hospitality

Core skills

Five credits.

Mandatory modules

Six credits.

This group covers working in a reception area, alcoholic beverages, cookery, silver service, hygiene practices, cleaning procedures and cleaning agents.

Optional modules
One credit.

The modules cover food preparation and cookery processes.

A pass in the additional assessment is also required.

Level III Hospitality

Core skills
Five credits.

Mandatory modules
Seven credits.

The modules include integrated production cookery, supervising people, integrated restaurant service, accommodation servicing, hotel reception, and cost and control in catering.

Optional modules
Six credits.

Students can choose from modules that develop skills and knowledge in the areas of meal and menu planning, linen and bedding services, personnel skills for supervisors, consumer studies, health and safety, and billing in the hotel and catering industry.

A pass in the additional assessment is also required.

Level II Information Technology

Core skills
Five credits.

Mandatory modules
Four credits.

The modules in this group provide an introduction to computer software, computer hardware, information technology in business and industry, and computer operating procedures.

Optional modules
Three credits.

Modules include computer application packages (database, spreadsheet and word processing), combinational logic, microcomputer hardware and programmable systems.

A pass in the additional assessment is also required.

Level III Information Technology

Core skills
Five credits.

Mandatory modules
Seven credits.

The modules cover computer programming and networks, operation and maintenance of computer hardware, and information systems.

Optional modules
Six credits from two of the following options – three from each:

- financial systems
- business systems
- software production
- technical support
- microtechnology
- knowledge systems
- mathematics.

A pass in the additional assessment is also required.

Level II Land-based Industries

Core skills
Five credits.

Mandatory modules
Three credits.

Modules cover accident and emergency procedures, animal anatomy and physiology, green plant and sustainable resource utilisation.

Optional modules
Four credits.

A broad range covering aspects of horticulture, forestry and agriculture.

A pass in the additional assessment is also required.

Level III Land-based Industries

Core skills
Six credits.

Mandatory modules
Three credits.

Modules cover science in context, health and safety in the work environment and sustainable resource utilisation.

Optional modules
Nine credits from one of the following options:

- ➡ horticulture
- ➡ forestry
- ➡ environment and conservation
- ➡ agriculture.

A pass in the additional assessment is also required.

Level II Leisure and Tourism

Core skills
Five credits.

Mandatory modules
Five credits.

The modules in this group provide an introduction to the field of leisure and tourism, first-aid measures, travel industry geography, maintaining financial records and recreation in the community.

Optional modules
Two credits from any of the following groups:

- ↦ sport and recreation
- ↦ travel services
- ↦ languages (18 foreign language modules available)
- ↦ business awareness (includes telephone skills, industrial relations, quality awareness, consumer studies and consumer law)
- ↦ design skills
- ↦ the Arts
- ↦ personal and social development (includes local investigations, work experience, and accident and emergency procedures).

A pass in the additional assessment is also required.

Level III Leisure and Tourism

Core skills
Five credits.

Mandatory modules
Five credits.

Included in this group are modules on the structure of the leisure and tourism industries respectively, the marketing of local tourist attractions, the management of customer care and financial record-keeping.

Optional modules
Eight credits from any of the following groups:

- → sport and recreation
- → supervisory skills
- → business awareness
- → design skills
- → languages (18 foreign language modules available)
- → the Arts (covering dance, drama and music-making)
- → personal and social development (includes work experience and practical investigations of people and the past, and people and the environment).

A pass in the additional assessment is also required.

Level II Science

Core skills
Five credits.

Mandatory modules
One credit in core mathematics.

Optional modules
Six credits, gained as follows:

- → three credits from the biology, chemistry or physics group
- → two credits from one of the other two science groups
- → one credit from any of the four groups.

The fourth optional group is very wide-ranging, with modules from biotechnology and microscopy to animal wildlife and wiring and assembly techniques.

A pass in the additional assessment is also required.

Level III Science – biology route

Core skills
Five credits.

Mandatory modules
Two credits.

The two modules cover statistics and experimental procedures in biology.

Optional modules
A total of 11 credits, gained as follows:

- ➥ four credits from the biology group
- ➥ two credits from either the chemistry group or the physics group
- ➥ five credits from any of the four groups.

The fourth optional group includes several mathematics modules, plus modules dealing with medical laboratory sciences, physiological measurement, cellular pathology, blood transfusion, clinical chemistry, biological control of pests and diseases, plant identification and computer application packages.

A pass in the additional assessment is also required.

Level III Science – chemistry route

Core skills
Five credits.

Mandatory modules
Two credits.

The two modules cover mathematics and experimental procedures in chemistry.

Optional modules
A total of 11 credits, gained as follows:

- ➥ four credits from the chemistry group

❧ two credits from either the biology group or the physics group

❧ five credits from any of the four groups.

Most of the modules in the fourth group deal with mathematics. The remaining modules in this group cover medical laboratory sciences, physiological measurements, pharmacology and computer application packages.

A pass in the additional assessment is also required.

Level III Science – physics route

Core skills
Five credits.

Mandatory modules
Two credits.

The two modules cover mathematics and experimental procedures in physics.

Optional modules
A total of 11 credits, gained as follows:

❧ four credits from the physics group

❧ two credits from either the chemistry group or the biology group

❧ five credits from any of the four groups.

Eight of the modules in the fourth group are concerned with mathematics. Among the other subjects covered in this group are: electronic component and circuit assembly techniques, semiconductor applications, logic families and digital systems analysis, electrostatics, electromagnetics, dynamics, simple harmonic motion and structure and properties of materials. One module covers computer application packages and information systems.

A pass in the additional assessment is also required.

Level II Technology

Core skills
Five credits.

Mandatory modules
Four credits.

The modules in this group cover accident and emergency procedures, employment law, roles and responsibilities within group business activity, quality awareness, and fundamentals of technology.

Optional modules
Either three credits from one of the following groups:

➻ construction
➻ engineering
➻ instrumentation and control
➻ information technology
➻ building services,

or one credit selected from each of three of the five optional groups listed above.

A pass in the additional assessment is also required.

Level III Technology

Core skills
Five credits.

Mandatory modules
Seven credits.

These modules cover work safety, industrial relations in the workplace, the individual in industry and work, Europe, quality assurance, measurement, graphical engineering communication and core mathematics.

Optional modules

Either six credits from one of the following options:

- construction
- engineering
- instrumentation and control
- information technology
- building services,

or two credits from each of three of the five optional groups listed above.

A pass in the additional assessment is also required.

Where can I find out more?

Full specifications will be available at your centre, or can be obtained from SCOTVEC. Their address is:

SCOTVEC
Hanover House
24 Douglas Street
Glasgow G2 7NQ
Tel: 0141-248 7900

Additional assessment

To achieve a GSVQ at levels II and III, you must pass an additional assessment as well as gaining the required number of module credits. There is no additional assessment for level I or Skillstart students. The additional assessment is also used to decide your grade for the full award. Individual modules are not graded.

The additional assessment is a project or assignment (eg a case-study, survey, report, etc) that is assessed by your teachers or other centre staff. Because it is meant to test your ability to draw together vocational and core skills from across the range of modules in your GSVQ, you will usually carry out the additional assessment towards the end of your programme.

Projects for the additional assessment can be devised by schools and colleges (or even by individual students), but they must be approved by SCOTVEC before use. Most GSVQ centres are using projects devised by the awarding body itself. Here are two sample additional assessment projects which meet the SCOTVEC requirements – the first from level II Arts and Social Sciences, the second from level III Technology.

Sample additional assessment project for level II Arts and Social Sciences students

The aim of the project is to examine whether and how a selected part of the mass media treats certain topics in a way that shows bias. In the course of the project candidates should:

- select a particular section of the mass media, eg a particular type of TV programme (serious political, news, documentary, soap, investigative, etc) or a particular style of newspaper, magazine, journal, comic book, etc
- select a particular topic, eg youth crime, Scottish nationalism, the monarchy, nuclear power, etc
- give an analysis of particular programmes or articles in their selected area that might be thought to show bias
- analyse a representative selection of programmes, articles, etc, in their selected area, to make a numerical estimate of the number of occasions when both sides of an issue are given equal coverage/time, and those occasions when they are not covered equally
- prepare a structured report of the project and its findings.

Sample additional project assessment for level III Technology students

The aim of the project is to demonstrate the potential of information technology in the context of a hypothetical company.

The candidate should imagine that he or she is employed as a computing technician in a small marketing firm with a total workforce of 22. The composition of this workforce is as follows:

- two partners who share the work of directing the firm
- nine marketing executives
- five administrative staff supervised by an office manager
- two graphics technicians
- a computing technician (this is the candidate)
- a telephonist/receptionist
- an office junior.

The hypothetical company should be imagined to have invested heavily in state-of-the-art information technology equipment in order to increase productivity.

Note that project supervisors should apply a detailed specification of the information technology equipment that has been bought by the hypothetical company, and supply the full range of technical data and supporting manuals for this equipment.

The candidate should imagine that he or she has been asked to demonstrate the potential of this equipment in the context of the work of the firm. In particular, the candidate has been asked to do the following:

- update the inventory database with details of the new information technology equipment acquired
- prepare an organisational structure chart and a brief description of the functions of the firm as a basis for discussing how information technology can be more widely used

➺ produce 'customised' instructions for end users using one major item of the equipment, including an outline of the action to be taken in the event of electrical repairs being required

➺ prepare an orthographic drawing of a workstation to accommodate a personal computer and printer

➺ create a spreadsheet for use in controlling a marketing project budget

➺ write a programme to calculate the monthly travel expenses of the marketing executives

➺ identify one further opportunity to demonstrate the potential of information technology equipment and prepare supporting material to illustrate that potential.

This information should be produced in the form of a report. The candidate will also be expected to make a verbal presentation of the main elements of the report to one of the partners (this should be carried out as a simulation). It is envisaged that contacts with real companies and other organisations will need to be made in producing the information required.

General requirements of additional assessment projects

Whatever additional assessment project you do, it must meet two basic requirements. It should:

1. require significant achievement on your part
2. allow you to demonstrate your skills in:

   ➺ planning
   ➺ implementation
   ➺ evaluation.

Significant achievement

Your project will cover a broad range of the subjects in your GSVQ, so it will take a fair amount of time to complete.

Expect a level II project to take around 20 hours in total, and a level III project to take up to 40 hours.

The actual modules that your project covers, together with a list of all the possible outcomes, will be listed in a project specification provided by your centre. At level II you should aim to achieve at least 12 outcomes, of which six to eight deal with practical skills and four to six cover underpinning skills, knowledge and understanding. At level III you should aim for a minimum of 18 outcomes, of which eight to 12 deal with practical skills and six to ten cover underpinning skills, knowledge and understanding.

Provided you strike this balance between the different kinds of skill, you can choose which particular outcomes to build into your project. You can, of course, seek guidance if necessary.

Planning

Once you understand the project specifications and have agreed what outcomes will be covered, you can start the planning phase. This begins with the preparation of a *project brief* that:

- → explains the specific aims of the project
- → lists the module outcomes to be covered
- → outlines the main stages of the project within a proposed timescale.

Planning stages

All projects will involve three main planning stages – 'preparation', 'doing' and 'feedback'. These should be described in your project brief, together with a proposed time of completion for each stage.

Preparation is a description of the things you will need before you can carry out the project. Obviously, requirements will vary from project to project, but usually you will require information and for many projects you will need materials, access to equipment, etc.

Doing is a list of all the things you must do to complete the project. This will include such activities as consulting sources, arranging visits, holding discussions, gathering data, writing reports, etc.

Feedback is a description of what you will do to check that you are carrying out your project along the correct lines. For example, if your project calls for you to produce a report, you might be expected to show a rough copy to a tutor before producing the final version. If your project involves organising an activity for a 'client', you might have to demonstrate the activity to a tutor or supervisor before trying it out for real.

Implementation

Implementation means meeting the specified aims of the project. You should follow the main stages and timescales as set out in your project brief.

Evaluation

Evaluation involves preparing a final report on your project. When producing the report, you should:

➼ indicate whether you have met the specified objectives in the project brief
➼ report on the way the stages and timescales were followed
➼ explain any problems you might have had, and list what steps you took to overcome these
➼ outline what you have learned from the project.

To give you some idea of how all these requirements are built into a project brief, here is another sample project, with a summary of the guidelines prepared by SCOTVEC. This project is from level II Care.

Sample additional assessment project for level II Care students

This project should be undertaken as part of a work placement or simulated work placement. The candidate is asked to design and implement a practical exercise that will enable clients to engage in creative activity (eg making a basket, cooking or baking, producing a jewellery box, a stool or some pottery). The activity chosen should involve a series of experiences over a period of time. The project should be carried out with a client group appropriate to the work placement, or with a suitable student or trainee group.

In designing and implementing the exercise, the candidate will need to:

- ensure that appropriate materials and equipment are available for the exercise
- ensure that the cost of the exercise is within the available budget
- produce written instructions (eg on the methods of construction that can be used) for the client to follow. The instructions may be largely pictorial in the case of certain client groups (eg young children, or people with learning difficulties)
- evaluate the benefits of the exercise to the client group and to the candidate
- where possible, use a computer and relevant software to produce the project report (or at least use a computer to produce some data, eg charts).

To satisfy the planning requirement for this project, your project brief should:

- include details of the client group and creative activity chosen
- list the module outcomes to be covered
- outline the main stages of the project from the starting point to completion, and propose a timescale.

Preparation for this project involves describing necessary resources – eg a catalogue of suitable materials and a budget for the materials.

Doing is a list of all the things to be done, in sequence. It will include:

➜ sources to consult
➜ meetings to arrange
➜ practising the activity
➜ demonstrating the activity to the client group
➜ assisting and encouraging the client group to carry out the activity
➜ collecting evidence.

These activities should be listed in sequence, with completion times for each one.

Feedback in this case will be a description of what has to be done to find out how suitable the proposed activity is for the client group. This will include:

➜ discussions with tutor or workplace supervisor
➜ discussions with the client group
➜ a practise session with members of the client group
➜ an account of whether and how the activity has been modified to take account of this feedback
➜ an account of the feedback gathered after the exercise has been carried out.

What the assessor is looking for

It is not essential in your additional assessment that you achieve in every detail all the individual outcomes covered by your project. Your assessors will be more interested in whether you met all or most of the aims described in your project brief. They will be looking for evidence of how successfully you integrated all the outcomes into the series of activities that make up your project. This evidence will be apparent from the way you planned, implemented and evaluated the project.

A chance to try again

You must pass the additional assessment project to gain the full GSVQ award at levels II and III. If you fail, you will of course be credited with all the modules you have already achieved, and you will be given another chance to pass the additional assessment. You can start with the same project specification if you want, but you must come up with a different project brief.

Assessing for final grade

Your project will be assessed to determine whether you should be awarded a Pass grade or a Merit grade. Before awarding a Merit grade, the assessors will want to be sure that you have consistently achieved higher standards than those set out in the project specification. In particular, they will be looking to see if you satisfy at least five of the following eight indicators:

1. You show initiative and high levels of motivation in planning, implementing and evaluating the project.
2. Your project as set out in your project brief involves a considerable degree of complexity in planning and implementation.
3. You set and achieve a demanding timescale for successful completion of the project.
4. You achieve high standards of personal and interpersonal skills.
5. You consistently demonstrate high standards of problem-solving skills in planning and carrying out the project.
6. You consistently show high standards of practical skills in carrying out the project.
7. The way in which you plan, implement and evaluate the project reveals consistent high standards in the area of underpinning skills, knowledge and understanding.
8. The way in which you plan, implement and evaluate the project demonstrates consistent evidence of flair in the handling of ideas and data.

If you don't achieve a Merit grade first time, you may be given the opportunity to try again, working to a different project brief.

Progression to employment, further training or higher education

 A student can come here having left school with four Standard grades and within four years they could complete a degree. They would do one year GSVQ, two years Higher National Diploma, and then a third year to convert that qualification into a degree.

A GSVQ tutor

Depending on what level you have achieved, you can go on to:

➤ a job
➤ a GSVQ at a higher level
➤ an occupational SVQ
➤ an HNC, HND, teacher-training course or degree.

Work

 A student with a GSVQ can't go to an employer and say with hand on heart: "I can do this job". But she can say: "I do know about this occupational area and I can do some of the tasks involved. Give me a little bit more training and I'll be a well-qualified and valuable employee."

A GSVQ tutor

National Certificate Modules are already highly regarded by many employers. Although GSVQs don't guarantee that you can do a particular job, the modules making up each award have been carefully grouped to cover the skills and knowledge that employers say they want in new recruits.

Certain groupings of modules in individual GSVQs are recognised as entry qualifications by a number of organisations. For example, certain groups of modules satisfy entry or recruitment requirements for teacher-training courses, administrative posts in the Civil Service and the Scottish Office, first-level nurse training, and the RAF.

Full details are given in the booklet *Recognised and Recommended Groupings of National Certificate Modules*, available free from SCOTVEC.

SVQs

Occupational SVQs (the equivalent of the NVQs offered elsewhere in the UK) meet standards set by industry and are accepted as proof of a person's ability to do a particular job. If you want to develop practical work skills in the area of your GSVQ, then occupational SVQs may be the logical next step. You will find the programmes easy to understand because they are designed along the same lines as GSVQs, and some occupational SVQs are made up of National Certificate Modules.

Higher National Certificate and Higher National Diploma

A pass in an appropriate level III GSVQ should satisfy the requirements for admission to HNC and HND courses. These qualifications, for students wishing to advance into professional and higher technical careers, are also awarded by SCOTVEC.

Level II GSVQ students can progress to HNC or HND provided that they gain additional credits in relevant modules.

Degree courses

For most GSVQ students, the route to a degree course would be as follows: level III – HNC or HND – conversion to degree. A level II award with additional credits can put you on the same path.

The Scottish Universities Council on Entrance (SUCE) recognises certain module groupings within GSVQs as the equivalent of Higher Grades. Some level III GSVQs allow you to gain the equivalent of up to four Higher Grade passes. Five Higher Grade passes at C or better are usually the minimum requirement for admission to a degree course, so you would normally need an additional Higher or equivalent qualification to satisfy the full entry requirements for a degree course.

Groupings recognised by the SUCE are listed in *Recognised and Recommended Groupings of National Certificate Modules*, available free from SCOTVEC. Remember, though, that individual higher education institutions set their own admission requirements, so check the acceptability of particular module groupings with the college or university of your choice.

7 GNVQs and Employment

Towards the end of their programme, the students do an assignment called "Where do I go from here?", which is a careers guidance project designed to help them decide where to go next – a job or Advanced GNVQ. If they choose to stay on, they can specialise in their preferred areas – sport or travel, for example. We point out all the options available, and the variety of additional units they can take.

A Leisure and Tourism tutor

This chapter takes a realistic look at two of the routes open to you when you have successfully completed a GNVQ programme.

It tells you:

- ↦ what the first GNVQ students planned to do
- ↦ how to progress up the GNVQ ladder
- ↦ how you can specialise in your GNVQ area
- ↦ why GNVQs can improve your employment prospects.

You will be interested to learn what the pioneering GNVQ students planned to do after completing the first programmes. In a survey covering just under 2,100 GNVQ students (about one-quarter of the first intake):

- ↦ nearly half intended to take advanced further education courses, mainly GNVQs at higher levels
- ↦ one-third hoped to progress into higher education
- ↦ 15 per cent intended taking NVQs
- ↦ six per cent of the students said that they planned to go directly into a full-time job.

This survey was conducted far too early to be a reliable guide to student destinations, but it does suggest that most students regard GNVQs as stepping stones to further or higher qualifications, rather than as pathways into full-time employment. Nearly four times as many students planned to go into higher education as into jobs. Since then these GNVQ students have gone through the application process for higher education. For information on their success, see chapter 8.

After your GNVQ

If you take a Foundation or Intermediate GNVQ, then a logical next step is to progress to a GNVQ at a higher level. By the time you are nearing the end of the one-year programme, you will know whether the vocational area is right for you, and you may have decided which particular aspects of the area you would like to explore more fully. You might also have a clear goal to aim for – a particular job you would like, or a higher education course you wish to join. In both cases, you should find out (if you do not already know) what additional qualifications might help you achieve your goal.

If you are an Advanced GNVQ student, you will probably have reached this decisive stage halfway through the two-year programme, by which time you should have completed (or be well on the way to completing) all the mandatory units. If you have not already done so, this is the time to tailor your programme to your particular needs.

Activity

At one college of further and higher education, Advanced students nearing the end of their first year are offered a list of provisional options for the second year. By then they should have completed their mandatory units and one of the optional units, 'Business information technology'. The options available to Advanced Business students at this particular centre are outlined below to indicate how a specific GNVQ can be extended and complemented. Other GNVQ centres will, of course, offer a different range of additional studies.

Second-year options for GNVQ Advanced Business students at one college centre

Option 1: you can take further GNVQ optional units or GNVQ additional units if you want to widen your GNVQ. You can choose from the following *optional units**:

- Marketing
- Business law
- European business
- Financial planning and control
- Personnel policies and procedures
- Behaviour at work
- Language unit (speaking and listening) in French, German or Spanish.

Additional units*:

- Document production
- Quantitative methods
- Financial accounting.

*The optional and additional units listed here are offered by a BTEC centre. Each awarding body sets its own optional and additional units, and each GNVQ centre chooses from the range available.

Option 2: you might want to follow parts of the NVQ if a clear career path is obvious to you. Two units are available:

- Accounting
- Business administration (secretarial).

You will have a strong foundation for achieving an NVQ because the structure of the programme is similar to GNVQ, with unit-based assessment procedures, compilation of evidence and responsibility for managing your own learning.

Option 3: you may want to improve your GCSE profile, particularly if you are interested in progression to higher education. GCSEs available are:

●▶ English
●▶ maths.

(Specify other subjects in which you are interested.)

Option 4: you might want to complement your GNVQ with an appropriate GCE A-level. The GCE A-levels available are:

●▶ economics
●▶ law
●▶ accounting
●▶ geography
●▶ English.

(Specify other subjects in which you are interested.)

Employment

Although only a small minority of students see a GNVQ as a direct route to employment, many students believe that the qualification will improve their employment prospects.

That confidence is probably well founded. The fact that you have a GNVQ should demonstrate to a prospective employer your practical interest in a vocational area. Your portfolio will provide evidence that you understand relevant skills and processes, and it will show sustained interest, ability and consistent output over a period of time. You might also have some relevant work experience.

GNVQ students say that their job prospects have been improved because their programmes have:

◆ made them better able to 'sell themselves' at interviews
◆ given them richness of experience compared with other students
◆ developed their self-confidence through managing their own learning
◆ made them familiar with working environments and practices.

Employers should welcome GNVQ applicants because the programmes develop a broad vocational knowledge, practical aptitudes and core skills that business and industry say they want, and that they feel are lacking in students with traditional academic qualifications.

Employment links

The majority of *large* employers are already familiar with NVQs, and as GNVQs become established, they too will become known to the majority of employers. Many organisations – from individual centres to the Confederation of British Industry (CBI) – are taking active steps to strengthen the links between GNVQs and the workplace. Initiatives include:

◆ Involving employers in GNVQs through organisations called TECs and Education Business Partnerships (EBPs).
◆ Developing close relationships with industry in order to deliver GNVQs. For example, a Huddersfield sixth-form college and Zeneca (formerly the pharmaceuticals division of ICI) are working together to deliver Manufacturing GNVQ. Teachers and company trainers produce course materials and assignments, and students' time is shared between college and workplace. All successful students have been guaranteed employment.

•• NCVQ and CBI working together to form GNVQ compacts between centres and employers at both local and national levels. These are similar to the compacts between centres and higher education institutions (page 199), with employers agreeing to interview all students with Advanced GNVQ in vocational areas relevant to their business. At national level, major companies will make this part of recruitment policy, and will familiarise their managers with GNVQs.

•• The Construction Industry Training Board (CITB) helping to develop teaching materials and assignments to support GNVQs.

•• The Banking Information Service (BIS) helping to co-ordinate a group of major employers working with schools. They are looking at the best ways to involve local employers in teaching the curriculum.

•• The Careers Service working with employers to gather information and arrange work experience. In South Derbyshire, the Careers Service and the TEC have devised a whole-school approach to integrated work experience with local employers.

GNVQs and Employment

The following passage was written by Ruth Jones. She is a Principal Advisor at NCVQ and leads the GNVQ Scholarship Scheme. She also works with the awarding bodies and other colleagues throughout the country to publicise GNVQs and to gain extra opportunities for GNVQ students to work with companies.

GNVQs are designed to provide a direct route to employment as well as to higher education. Although in the early days most students thought mainly in terms of progressing to higher education, new opportunities are opening up as employers are rapidly becoming familiar with the new qualifications.

Information will soon be available to students and career teachers on the relevant NVQ qualifications that students can progress to on completing a GNVQ in any subject area. Some students are already following programmes which include units of more job-specific NVQs, often supported by local employers who have developed NVQ programmes for their own staff. Most GNVQ students are likely to find their studies a good preparation for future employment, although the earliest job-seekers should be prepared to sell the strong points of their new qualifications themselves!

Until recently employers had not heard much about the new qualifications. Few students have as yet finished their courses; of those that have, many have progressed to higher education. However, as the first GNVQ students prepare to enter the world of work, NCVQ and partners at local and national levels are working hard to familiarise the qualifications. The Employment Department has brought out a leaflet which has been sent to all major employers, backed up with an employers information pack. Students can also take this leaflet to an interview, or even send it in with the application form.

NCVQ and partners in education and industry have also launched a new scheme to encourage national and local employers to support and recognise GNVQs. Eleven international companies to date are supporting the new GNVQ Scholarship Scheme, which offers help for GNVQ students during their courses, with company awards to the best students. Companies provide opportunities for work experience, gateways for possible future employment and learning materials. The following companies are offering support in the following areas:

McDonalds (Business); Hilton National (Hospitality and Catering); American Express (Leisure and Tourism);

*J Laing plc (Construction and the Built Environment);
Vidal Sassoon (Art and Design); Sainsbury's (GNVQ Core
Skills); Girobank (Business); The Post Office (Business);
The National Health Service Directorate (Health and
Social Care); United Biscuits (Manufacturing) and
Peugeot (Business).*

*Other companies are coming on board rapidly. All of the
sponsor companies are keen to support the scheme because
they think that GNVQs will provide them with a better
workforce, whether students join them before or after
higher education. Vidal Sassoon, for instance, will offer
employment to their successful scholars in Art and Design
GNVQ. Sainsbury's will make an overall award linked to
vacation work for students going on to higher education in
a related subject.*

*Other companies are also supporting NVQ students
because the qualification provides a good grounding for
future company training. Zeneca, for instance, offers bur-
saries and final offers of employment to successful GNVQ
Manufacturing students.*

*Employers are involved in the design and creation of
GNVQs, in line with the country's future need for a com-
petitive workforce. GNVQs are proving attractive to
employers for well-founded reasons. When applying for
jobs, successful GNVQ students can be confident that the
knowledge and skills they have acquired will be valued.*

Major employers welcome the fact that GNVQs give students a broad understanding of the nature and aims of businesses

*The National Health Service Training Directorate, for
instance, considered that GNVQs afforded students
'invaluable knowledge and understanding of a broad
employment sector' whilst American Express thought that
GNVQs provide 'a sound preparation for working life as*

well as a valuable new route into higher education'. Sainsbury's considered GNVQs 'a practical and relevant qualification for many young people to start their careers.'

Employers also welcomed the personal qualities encouraged by GNVQs

GNVQ students manage their own learning, must research and analyse issues for themselves and must evaluate and improve their own performance. They must learn to work in teams as well as individually.

> *GNVQs encourage students to go out and find answers for themselves. They are designed to foster enterprise and initiative – people who can set their own goals and achieve them, yet know how to pull together as a team to achieve results. Employees who can combine knowledge and theory with "common sense".*

Michael Heron, Chairman of NCVQ and Chairman of the Post Office

The GNVQ core skills also provide students with basic skills needed by all employers

Employees who are skilled in information handling, can use computers and possess good communication and number skills are valuable in all businesses.

David Sainsbury, Chief Executive of J Sainsbury's plc, summed up the views of many employers.

> *The strength of a GNVQ lies in the way that it combines an understanding of the world of business with the proven acquisition of core skills.*

'We need good communication skills to better serve our customers and to establish effective working relationships. The ability to detect trends and to relate figures to each other is covered by Application of Number. We are also increasingly dependent on computers and need employees who can understand them and put them to good effect. We

also need a strong sense of teamwork, in-house and across the company, if we are to make effective use of resources, hence the importance of working with others.

'With an ever-increasing pace of change we will not survive unless our people are motivated to increase their own performance and have a problem-solving approach. If we can employ people with these skills our business will be all the more effective and hence we are keen to support the introduction of GNVQs.

These employers are not alone. Schools and colleges report that small and medium-sized companies all over the country are beginning to offer support for GNVQ students and their teachers, often as part of local charters or compacts whereby both students and employers sign mutual pledges. Local Training and Enterprise Councils, Education–Business Partnerships and a host of organisations supporting education–business links are all working together to involve local employers. As GNVQs are also making regular headlines in the national press, the chances are that in the very near future most employers, including recruitment staff, will both recognise and value your new qualification.

8 GNVQs and Access to Higher Education

This chapter tells you what you need to know about GNVQs as entry qualifications for universities and other higher education institutions (HEIs).

It tells you:

- about HE courses in subjects that may lead from your vocational programme
- what your university prospects are
- how GNVQ centres are creating links with higher education institutions
- how to find out the entry requirements of universities and other HEIs
- how to enhance the value of your GNVQ.

Higher education

Higher National Certificate and Higher National Diploma

BTEC, one of the three GNVQ-awarding bodies, offers the Higher National Certificate and the Higher National Diploma. These are modular programmes leading to qualifications that are considered to be just below degree standard, but which are highly regarded by employers. They provide one route of progression for Advanced GNVQ students or equivalent who wish to acquire nationally recognised qualifications for higher technical, managerial and supervisory posts in the fields of:

- Built Environment
- Business and Finance and Public Administration
- Computing and Information Systems

➡ Design
➡ Distribution, Hotel and Catering and Leisure Services
➡ Engineering
➡ Land and Countryside
➡ Science and Caring.

These umbrella titles include many vocational subjects. In Design alone, for example, you can choose from more than 40 courses, covering all aspects of Design from Advertising and Architectural Stained Glass to Three-Dimensional Studies and Typography.

The minimum entry requirement is one GCE A-level plus supporting GCSEs (English and maths), or equivalent, so Advanced GNVQ students should have no difficulty gaining entry. If you are already taking a GNVQ at a college which offers BTEC courses, then there is a good chance that the Higher National that you may wish to take is available at the same centre. The Higher National Certificate is a two-year, part-time course that you can take on day-release, block-release or at evening classes. The Higher National Diploma is a two-year, full-time, or a three-year, part-time, course. On completion, it might be possible to transfer to a degree course.

Another potential route to a degree is the Diploma of Higher Education. As a two-year, non-vocational course, the Diploma was introduced for prospective teachers, but now caters for a wider group of students. It is equivalent to the first two years of a degree course, but it lacks a strong identity, so most students go on to further studies, mainly degree courses.

Degree courses

Most of the GNVQ Advanced students who were offered conditional places at HEIs in 1993 and were accepted for degree courses had additional qualifications – either additional GNVQ units or one or more GCE A/AS-levels.

But to show how GNVQ on its own can open doors, here's Eleanor's story. Eleanor, who was one of the first Advanced Health and Social Care students, also took GCE A-level sociology.

Eleanor's Story

At the end of the first year of my programme, I went to university open days and asked if they would take Advanced GNVQ as an entry qualification for a midwifery degree. Some didn't, some weren't sure, and a few didn't even know what a GNVQ was. The question they kept asking me was: "Do you have any A-levels to go with it?"

'At that stage I got discouraged and seriously asked myself if there was any point in going on with my programme. But my teachers told me that by the time I applied for places, the universities would have a better idea of the value of GNVQs, and since it was too late to do another A-level, I decided to finish the programme.

'In September I applied for degree courses at six universities. [Eleanor's choice of institutions was divided equally between old and new universities.] Three of them turned me down, one said my application would only be considered if I was a Registered General Nurse, and the two others [one in Yorkshire, the other in Lancashire] offered me interviews.

'Unfortunately, on the day I was meant to go to Yorkshire, there was a blizzard and I couldn't make it. They said they offered me another interview, but I never received the letter, and by the time I got in touch the offer had been withdrawn. So that left me with only one chance.

'I went up to the Lancashire interview with my dad and my sister. We got lost several times and by the time I arrived, they'd already started the group interview. Apart from looking bad, I'd missed the explanation of the course, so my prospects didn't look too bright.

'At my individual interview, there were two people questioning me to begin with. They didn't know much about GNVQ and I had to explain everything from scratch. I'd taken up my portfolio with three vocational units and a core skills element and I used them to talk through my programme.

'Then one of the interviewers went through my portfolio. She couldn't believe it! She thought GNVQ was a wonderful course and asked lots of questions about it. I felt really good afterwards.

'When the university wrote, they offered me a place if I got a Pass at Advanced. I'd explained about the different grades and said I hoped to get a Distinction, but they were happy with a Pass. They didn't even say I had to get my A-level.

Raising awareness

Don't be alarmed by Eleanor's rather disheartening experience at her university open days. Since then, awareness of GNVQs among HEIs has been raised considerably thanks to initiatives by NCVQ, by the Universities and Colleges Admission Service (UCAS), and by many individual GNVQ centres.

NCVQ, aware that the credibility of GNVQ depends on its being accepted for progression to both employment and higher education, has set up a project called 'GNVQs and Access to Higher Education' (GATE). Managed by UCAS and NCVQ, GATE interprets GNVQs for higher education staff and provides feedback to schools and colleges in the form of likely admissions requirements. GATE's initiatives include:

➹ compiling a database giving higher education institutions' criteria for GNVQ candidates' entry
➹ providing information on GNVQs to HEIs and admissions tutors through conferences and workshops

- ➦ supplying information to NCVQ on the awareness and perception of GNVQs among HE admissions tutors
- ➦ providing advice to GNVQ centres about progression to higher education
- ➦ monitoring the progress of Advanced GNVQ students applying to HEIs through UCAS
- ➦ tracking GNVQ students during their higher education courses.

Many GNVQ centres have independently established mutually beneficial links with HE institutions. Called compacts, links or partnerships, these initiatives generally raise awareness of GNVQs and also offer the HE institutions opportunities to take an active part in the delivery of GNVQ programmes. More than 100 GNVQ centres are already in compacts and more are planned.

Compact initiatives

'We had already talked to the [HE college] staff about possible progression from Advanced GNVQ onto their BA and BEd courses,' reported one GNVQ centre. 'We went

back to them again and asked them if they would like to help us to develop and deliver GNVQ Leisure and Tourism.'

The centre explained the advantages of such a partnership. 'The GNVQ students would have access to extensive facilities, would be taught by experts in leisure and tourism and have the experience of working with higher education students who would provide valuable role models...the involvement would give prestige to the course and add to the credibility of the qualification.'

Encouraged by the success of this compact, the centre decided to branch out. 'We are now considering expanding the links with higher education by exploring a partnership with Plymouth University's Tourism course.'

Another centre described the benefits it had derived from the wide-ranging compacts it had forged with four universities. 'They range from guarantees of interviews to all students achieving Advanced GNVQ, to involvement in the teaching of our programmes and marking of work leading to guaranteed access to higher education courses. We are seeking to make further similar links.'

HE institutions' attitudes to GNVQs

If your centre doesn't have this type of link-up with HE, don't worry that you'll be left at a disadvantage when it comes to applying for courses. Many HE institutions have information about GNVQs and have stated that they recognise the Advanced award as a suitable entry qualification. Individual universities' and HE colleges' policy towards Advanced GNVQ is set out in GATE's regularly updated database.

By the middle of 1992, 102 HE colleges and universities had accepted Advanced GNVQ as a suitable access qualification. Of these, about 30 guaranteed interviews to all first phase GNVQ candidates, while many of the HE institutions involved in compacts pledged to interview candidates from participating centres. About 70 institutions hadn't indicated their position on GNVQs, and seven – mainly medical and dental schools – said that the award didn't satisfy their entry requirements.

Of the HE institutions that accept Advanced GNVQ for degree courses, all but a few ask for additional qualifications – either additional GNVQ units or a GCE A/AS-level. Many also set the condition that candidates should achieve GNVQ at Merit or Distinction grade.

These conditions aren't unduly stiff. A GNVQ Pass is generally regarded as more challenging than two low grade GCE A-levels because of the demands made by core skills achievement. Just as GCE A-level applicants need more than two passes to get on to popular courses, so GNVQ students will need additional performance for places on courses where demand is greater than supply.

It works both ways, though. Higher education institutions want to fill the places on the courses they offer, and if these courses don't attract sufficient applications from candidates with the specified entry qualification, the university or HE college may lower the requirements.

General requirements of individual HE colleges and universities are listed in the GATE database mentioned above and are available from NCVQ.

When asked about preferred additional qualifications:

- 44 HE institutions were willing to accept either a GCE A-level, AS or additional GNVQ units
- HE institutions with a usual entry requirement of three GCE A-levels at A or B grades often required Advanced GNVQ with a Distinction grade, plus a high grade in a GCE A-level covering a different subject.

To find out the precise requirements of a particular degree course, you or your careers adviser should refer to the HEI prospectus, the *CRAC Degree Course Guides*, which from April 1995 contain information on GNVQ entry requirements, the University and College Entrance (UCE) Guide and the GATE database. If these don't supply the answers you're looking for, telephone either the GATE database through the NCVQ Information Line (0171-728 1843) or the appropriate HEI contact.

Entry conditions for different courses offered by the same institution may vary. For example, one university accepts a GNVQ at Merit for entry to its Manufacturing course, while access to the same university's Business Studies course requires a Distinction plus six additional units or a GCE A-level at grade B. By contrast, another university accepts Manufacturing candidates only if they have a Distinction plus one or more GCE A/AS-levels in maths/physics.

As explained above, variations such as these often reflect the different level of demand for places. Some HE institutions have difficulty recruiting students on to some courses, while others can select from a large number of applicants, many of whom will have qualifications well above the minimum requirements.

How to enhance your GNVQ programme

Even if you have not decided which HE course you want to follow after GNVQ, you should be aware of the different ways in which you can tailor your post-16 programme to suit your own aims and abilities. There are five ways in which you can enhance the value of your GNVQ:

- by working towards a Merit or Distinction grade
- by taking additional GNVQ units
- by taking a suitable GCE A-level or AS-level that may complement and extend the scope of your GNVQ

♦ by resitting GCSE maths and/or English if you have not achieved A–C grades in these subjects

♦ by taking one or more of the three optional core skills, or by achieving a higher level in the mandatory core skills.

Making the grade

The GNVQ grading system is fully explained in chapter 1. One of the advantages of GNVQ over GCE A-levels is that you should have the opportunity to improve your grade throughout your programme, so if you are offered a place conditional on getting a Merit grade, you will have several months to bring your work up to the required standard.

GNVQ grades are awarded for the general skills – planning, information seeking, information handling and evaluation – which go into the work. GNVQs are also graded on a theme called 'quality of outcomes'. Chapter 1 explains how this works. In most vocational areas, students who are good at these skills will usually produce finished work of a matching standard, but in Art and Design, which includes personal creative work, it is possible that a student with a Pass grade may actually have a stronger art portfolio than a student who has been awarded a Distinction.

HE colleges offering art and design courses recognise the problem and, where encouraged by a tutor's report or reference, would ask to see the candidate's portfolio. Some colleges also ask suitable candidates to submit a video or audio tape presenting their work.

Additional GNVQ units

At many centres you will be offered the chance to take up to six additional units; adding six units to your Advanced GNVQ increases its challenge to roughly three GCE A-levels. You can make up this package with special additional units, more optional units from the same vocational area, or mandatory vocational units from another area. As yet, none of the special additional units has been accredited by NCVQ, but most HE institutions recognise them as entrance qualifications. Some institutions take GNVQ grades into account and set entry requirements accordingly – for example, asking for either an Advanced award at Distinction, or a GNVQ Merit plus six additional units.

When putting together a package of additional units, it is advisable to choose some units from different vocational areas. As a senior educationalist explained: 'If I were an admissions tutor, I would be looking for additional units that offered something extra.... I would be saying to myself: the mandatory and optional units offer a certain amount of evidence for coverage of a particular area. I would therefore expect the additional units to do two things: to extend the area covered, and also to extend the range of relevant evidence and the way it is assessed.'

For some courses, it is advisable to target particular areas outside your basic programme. For example, Health and Social Care students intending to take a nursing course are advised to choose additional units based on biological science. Leisure and Tourism candidates wishing to take a degree course involving modern languages will need language competence acquired either through GNVQ units or other studies.

GCE A-levels

For degree courses in science and engineering, many HE institutions require additional evidence of ability in maths as a basic entry requirement. Some HEIs say that additional GNVQ maths units meet this requirement, but others will be looking for GCE A/AS-levels. At some of the older universities, where GCE A-level candidates will be expected to have good passes in three subjects, the basic entry requirement for GNVQ candidates for all degree courses is an Advanced award plus one GCE A-level.

If you want to give yourself the widest choice of HE courses, the GCE A/AS-level option is worth considering; you will have more than one card to play. The GNVQ will show that you have the relevant skills and the ability to manage your own learning, while the GCE A-level shows that you are capable of applying analytical skills. You might also choose to take a GCE A-level because you want to keep up a favourite subject, or because it will extend your career options.

Usually you would take one suitable GCE A-level or two AS courses. Some exceptional students are taking two GCE A-levels with their advanced GNVQ, but this package is very demanding and should not be regarded as the norm. HE institutions do not expect GNVQ candidates to have more than one GCE A-level. In the pilot phase, when GNVQs' acceptability as an HE entry qualification was less clear, some GNVQ students decided to play safe by taking two GCE A-levels but students found the workload too heavy and fell behind with their GNVQ programme. When they applied for HE courses, the HEIs not surprisingly also played safe and offered them places conditional on passing the two GCE A-levels. In effect, the HEIs treated them as GCE A-level applicants, and as a result, the students stopped work on their GNVQ programmes to concentrate on getting good GCE A-level grades.

A GCE A-level that complements and extends your GNVQ will probably be rated more highly than one that covers similar ground. Maths would make a valuable addition to any GNVQ, and a foreign language is always an asset. As with additional units, check the HE institution's preferences for a particular course with your careers adviser, the HEI's prospectus, UCE or the GATE database.

Core skills and GCSE

Check the GCSE English and maths requirement of the HE course you want to follow. Some HEIs ask for a C grade or higher in these subjects. If you haven't got these grades, you might find that credits in the core skills Application of Number and Communication are not enough to meet the entry requirement. In any case, it's worth trying to improve your GCSE grades in these important subjects.

Additional core skills credits can strengthen your application. You can either achieve the mandatory core skills at a higher level, or take one or more of the recommended core skills.

Selling yourself

GNVQ tutors are confident that many of their students are better able than GCE A-level candidates to talk clearly about what they have learned from their programmes. 'They have clearer aims than the average GCE A-level student,' said one teacher, 'and a better perception of the world outside school.'

It's partly up to you to put across the value of your GNVQ programme. First, make the best use of the 'Personal Statement' section of the UCAS application form. Explain why you chose GNVQ and what you have achieved from your studies. Explain how your programme has prepared you for your chosen HE course, your background interest in the subject and what insights you have gained from your out-of-school activities. Emphasise what you have *learned*, rather than what you have *done*.

There's a possibility that you'll be able to expand on this at an interview. Some HEIs are keen to see GNVQ candidates to assess the calibre of the new qualification. Others – mainly those involved in compacts – guarantee an interview to all Advanced GNVQ candidates. However, not all are able to do so because of the large number of applicants.

If you are offered an interview (for a job or a place on an educational course), make the most of it. Treat the event as another assignment with a particular outcome to be achieved, and prepare a plan of action to help you achieve it. You may have conducted interviews yourself as part of your GNVQ programme, and you will probably have gained a good practical knowledge of interviewing techniques. You should have also developed some of the important qualities – self-motivation, communication skills, confidence, organisation – that the interviewer(s) will be seeking.

Take along a small sample of your best work, highlighting assignments of relevance to the proposed course. Don't expect the interviewer to study your entire portfolio, however impressive it may be. Content is important, as is presentation. One of the reasons why Eleanor made such a good impression was that her portfolio was beautifully organised and designed. All her material was clearly cross-referenced and written in a neat and legible hand. She made good use of painstakingly drawn illustrations and charts. Even before her interviewers had read one word, they must have known that here was a candidate who not only worked hard on her GNVQ projects, but also enjoyed them and set herself high standards. Competence and enthusiasm make a winning team.

Glossary of Terms

Accredited units: GNVQ units that have been approved by the National Council for Vocational Qualifications (NCVQ).

Additional units: units that can be taken by students who wish to extend their vocational knowledge and enhance the value of their GNVQ. Each awarding body offers its own additional units.

Assessment: the regular evaluation of a student's work to see if it meets the specified requirements. Assessment is carried out by members of staff and is also used to determine final grades.

Certificate: the document, issued by the awarding bodies, that lists the units that a student has successfully achieved.

Compact: a link between a GNVQ centre or centres and one or more higher education institutions.

Core skills/core skills units: skills that are considered essential in all walks of life. Communication, Application of Number and Information Technology are mandatory core skills units in all GNVQs. GNVQ students are also encouraged to develop Problem-solving and Personal Skills.

Element: a subdivision of a unit, identifying the skills, knowledge and understanding that students must achieve.

Evidence: the material gathered by GNVQ students and submitted for assessment against the requirements for each unit. Evidence may be presented in many forms, such as written reports, video tapes, sketches and drawings; and it can be generated by a wide range of planned activities, including case-studies, surveys, work experience, role-play, etc.

Evidence indicators: the general forms in which evidence must be presented (report, case-study, etc) to demonstrate that the unit requirements have been met.

Grades/grading: GNVQs are awarded as Pass, Merit or Distinction. The award of Merit and Distinction grades is based upon an assessment of the overall body of work collected by a student in the course of a GNVQ programme. At least one-third of the work must exceed the basic requirements for a Pass.

Grading criteria: the range of skills – planning, information seeking and information handling, evaluation and quality of outcomes – that are assessed to grade a GNVQ award as Pass, Merit or Distinction.

Individual action plan (IAP): a goal-setting plan drawn up by a student. It takes into account previous achievements, aspirations and abilities. A student (with a tutor's help) would create an IAP on entry to a GNVQ programme.

Induction programme: an introductory course offered by schools and colleges to familiarise students with the structure and requirements of their GNVQ programme.

Integrated skills: skills applied in a practical context.

Mandatory units: a specified number of vocational and core skills units that all GNVQ students must take to achieve the full award. The number of mandatory vocational units is different for each GNVQ level, but at all levels there are three mandatory core skills units.

National Council for Vocational Qualifications (NCVQ): the organisation which, together with the three awarding bodies, ensures that the standards for GNVQs are maintained.

National framework of qualifications: a proposed system of qualifications – GNVQs, NVQs, GCE A-levels, etc – linked within a national framework that shows the comparable levels of vocational and academic qualifications and indicates how students may take different pathways to reach similar goals.

National Record of Achievement (NRA): a national system, adopted by the majority of schools, for recording a student's qualifications and achievements through to higher education and beyond. It is proposed that the NRA will include a provision for individual action planning to help students identify and attain their goals.

Optional units: a range of vocational units from which students select a certain number for each GNVQ level.

Performance criteria: a list of the things that must be done in order to satisfy the requirements for an element.

Portfolio of Evidence: the collection of material submitted by a student for assessment.

Programme: the GNVQ course.

Range: different settings or situations in which evidence should be gathered.

Specification: see **Unit specifications.**

Tests: see **Unit end tests.**

Unit: the smallest part of a GNVQ qualification that can be accredited by the awarding bodies. GNVQs are made up of vocational units and core skills units, and these are mandatory, optional or additional.

Unit end tests: short-answer or multiple-choice questions designed to test a student's knowledge and understanding in the areas covered by the vocational units. Tests for the mandatory vocational units are set by the awarding bodies; optional and additional units are tested by GNVQ centres.

Unit specifications: the precise requirements of each unit, listing elements, performance criteria, range and evidence indicators. Specifications for the mandatory vocational units and core skills units are the same for any given GNVQ, irrespective of the awarding body.

Verification: the process by which assessments are checked for consistency and fairness. Verification is carried out by internal verifiers appointed by GNVQ centres. The awarding bodies also verify assessments to see that they meet the national standards for GNVQs.

Vocational area: loosely speaking, the subject matter of a GNVQ, covering the general skills, processes and knowledge relevant to a range of related occupations.

Vocational units: units identifying different areas of competence within the general vocational area. Vocational units may be mandatory, optional or additional.

Index